AMERICAN VIOLENCE

RICHARD MAXWELL BROWN is Professor of History at
The College of William and Mary and author of *The
South Carolina Regulators*, a study of America's first
major vigilante movement. In 1968–69 he served as a
consultant to the National Commission on the Causes
and Prevention of Violence. In that connection, he
contributed an article, "Historical Patterns of Violence
in America," and a monograph, "The American Vigilante Tradition," to *Violence in America: Historical
and Comparative Perspectives: A Report to the National Commission on the Causes and Prevention of
Violence*, edited by Hugh Davis Graham and Ted
Robert Gurr.

AMERICAN VIOLENCE

Edited by
RICHARD MAXWELL BROWN

Prentice-Hall, Inc. *Englewood Cliffs, N.J.*

A SPECTRUM BOOK

Current printing (last number):

10 9 8 7 6 5 4 3 2 1

PRENTICE-HALL INTERNATIONAL, INC. (*London*)
PRENTICE-HALL OF AUSTRALIA, PTY. LTD. (*Sydney*)
PRENTICE-HALL OF CANADA, LTD. (*Toronto*)
PRENTICE-HALL OF INDIA PRIVATE LIMITED (*New Delhi*)
PRENTICE-HALL OF JAPAN, INC. (*Tokyo*)

To my wife

CONTENTS

ACKNOWLEDGMENTS

I offer my grateful thanks to the staff of the Earl Gregg Swem Library of The College of William and Mary for their incalculable assistance in the preparation of this book. I wish to acknowledge, also, the contribution of my students at William and Mary who have joined me in the study of American violence: in particular, Sally James, Michael Chesson, Bruce Stanley, Mary Ann Mason, Pamela Baldwin, and Barbara Crissey. My greatest debt, as always, is to my wife.

AMERICAN VIOLENCE

Introduction

Violence has formed a seamless web with the most positive episodes in American history: the birth of the nation (Revolutionary violence), the freeing of the slaves and the preservation of the Union (Civil War violence), the occupation of the land (Indian wars), the stabilization of frontier society (vigilante violence), the elevation of the farmer and the laborer (agrarian and labor violence), and the preservation of law and order (police violence). The patriot, the humanitarian, the nationalist, the pioneer, the farmer, the laborer, and the capitalist have all used violence as an ignoble means to a noble end.

Goal-oriented in nature, American violence has often been conservative in its assertion of community values and defensive of the interests of established social and economic blocs and local groups. Rising elements like the urban Irish, the laboring masses, and the ghetto blacks have also employed violence to gain larger shares of the privileges and benefits of American society. Although we have seldom included it in our explicit system of values, our frequent resort to violence has established it as a crucial factor in our real but unacknowledged value structure.

American violence antedates the American nation. Most of the major types of our violent activity were well established before we gained our independence from Great Britain. Urban violence appears as far back as the *Boston uprising against Governor Andros in 1689*.[1] Racial violence is as ancient as the *New York City slave uprisings of 1712* and 1741 and South Carolina's Stono Rebellion of 1739. Agrarian violence by white men broke out in such insurgencies as that of the Virginia tobacco planters, who followed Nathaniel Bacon in rebellion in 1676. The first settlers at Jamestown quickly became embroiled in conflict with the Indians. Frontier conflict among white men was exemplified by America's first significant vigilante movement, the *South Carolina Regulators of 1767–69*. The urban riot—for which there was ample precedent in the British Isles of the seventeenth and eighteenth centuries—was seen in such instances as the *Boston impressment riot of*

---

[1] Italicized items are represented by documents in this book.

1747. No less important was the rural riot, of which the New Jersey land riots of 1745–55 furnished many examples.

The colonial period was climaxed by an event of staggering significance in the history of American violence: the Revolution. The war for American independence began largely as a movement of violent urban resistance to British policy beginning with the *Stamp Act riots of 1765* and continuing through the fateful *Boston Tea Party of 1773*. With the actual outbreak of fighting in 1775 the main theater of violence in the war years moved to the countryside as thousands of rural Americans flocked to enlist in the Continental Army of Washington and joined in the local guerrilla strife with the British and the Tories that boiled from the Hudson to the Savannah and was especially severe in South Carolina. Aside from the fact that violence was a *sine qua non* for gaining independence, the Revolution was the supreme lesson to Americans that in practical terms violence pays. For many later generations the Revolution legitimized violence when used for what was deemed a good cause. The Revolutionary heritage of violence has been invoked again and again. One example is the *anti-rent movement in upstate New York,* whose members in the 1840s disguised themselves as Mohawks when committing violence against landlords and officers in conscious emulation of the precedent of the Boston Tea Party.

Violence accelerated in the nineteenth century. *During the 1830s, 1840s, and 1850s a wave of urban riots flayed the nation.* The turbulence was especially acute in the growing metropolises of the northeast, but it stretched to the new cities of the Mississippi Valley as well. The wave of urban violence in the early nineteenth century drives home the point that "the problem of the city" is an old one in American history. A complex intermingling of economic, political, ideological, racial, ethnic, and religious tensions led to urban violence in a pattern that portended the urban strife of today. While the people in our cities rioted repeatedly, the rapid westward movement of the frontier spread *the vigilante impulse*—basic to the American proclivity for extralegal violence in support of community values—to the corners of the nation. And while the country still reeled from urban riots and vigilante violence, Americans in the middle of the nineteenth century were engulfed in an orgy of violence: the Civil War. In addition to the staggering number of military casualties, both the North and the South were torn by guerrilla violence, bushwhacking, and civil strife behind the lines. Notable in this connection was the massive *anti-draft riot in New York City in 1863.* Violence traceable to tensions originating in the Civil War lasted until the closing years of the nineteenth century. Such movements as *the Ku Klux Klan, the Molly Maguires,* the Bald Knobbers, and *the family feuding of the southern mountains* and the southwest dated, in part, to Civil War animosities. The period from the Civil War to World War I was probably the most violent one in our history. Urban and frontier violence flourished as before while labor violence—hand in hand with the rapid expansion of American industrialization after the Civil War—entered a new era of explosiveness with the *great railroad strike of 1877;* the strike actually reached an insurrectionary level *in Pittsburgh.* Racial violence had not been quiescent since the colonial slave uprisings—the greatest black rebellion was *Nat Turner's in 1831*—but after the Civil War took a new form in the lynching of thousands of Southern black people in support of an iron-clad system of white supremacy.

Local violence was pervasive in the period from the Civil War to World War I. Virtually all areas of the land were plagued with bands of violent citizens—Bulldozers in Mississippi, Dynamiters in Ohio, *White Caps in Indiana* and elsewhere, *Night Riders in Kentucky,* to mention but a few. The reasons for the rise of the local movements of violence were almost as numerous as the hundreds of them that appeared, but generally the movements seem to have been local responses to major shifts in the nation's development, such as the transition from a rural to an urban society. Most of the local movements sprang up in the countryside and in the small towns—the parts of America that were being eclipsed by booming urbanization. The social and economic anxieties thereby released often found vent in violence. Such was the case in western Kentucky from 1906 to 1908, when economically depressed tobacco planters turned to Night Rider violence to break the strangle hold of monopolistic buyers on the market.

Details differ but many of the patterns remain the same in our own era of violence. Although the twentieth century has seen the transition from the *"communal"* race riot (whites and blacks killing each other) to the *"commodity"* race riot (blacks destroying property), the convergence of urban and racial violence that is typical of our age was apparent as early as the New York slave uprising of 1712. The decade of the 1960s has been unparalleled for the number of assassinations of leading public figures (John F. Kennedy, Robert F. Kennedy, Martin Luther King, Jr., Malcolm X, Medgar Evers, George Lincoln Rockwell), but the presidential assassin as a type (*i.e.,* a person of basic mental instability with a superficial ideological orientation) is consistent from *Charles Guiteau,* killer of Garfield, and *Leon Czolgosz,* killer of McKinley, to *Lee Harvey Oswald,* killer of Kennedy. With the upsurge in urban riots, racial violence, and assassination, it is sometimes difficult to remember that frontier and labor violence have faded from the scene. Yet the bitter fruits of such upheavals remain with us, for the continuing tendency to violence owes much to the impact of both of them. Meanwhile, most Americans have paid little heed to an evil that has been growing since early in the century—*organized crime* —by which means increasingly large sectors of legitimate commercial enterprise are being taken over by racketeers. With the people apathetic and the politicians indifferent, "the business of violence" dangerously threatens the nation's health.

Where are we bound? The majority of Americans seem to feel that our institutions are strong and resilient enough to transcend, ultimately, the present wave of violence. But there is a cautionary example in the recent case of Colombia and its *violencia* which flared in the late 1940s, reached its peak in the 1950s, and is not wholly extinguished today. Colombia in 1946 was one of the most stable of the South American republics; hence there was little reason to expect the ensuing catastrophe. What began as an acute political conflict soon degenerated into a general phenomenon, the *violencia*—mindless banditry, murder, torture, and anarchy in which hundreds of thousands of Colombians perished during the 1940s and 1950s. The specter of the *violencia* is a sobering one, for our present social problems are in many ways as formidable as those that inflamed Colombia two decades ago.

We have always had a good deal of confidence in our ability to deal peacefully with our problems, no matter how serious; but in recent years our optimism has been shaken. The period from 1940 to the late 1950s was one of the least violent eras in our history. To many Americans it seemed that large-scale violence had come to an end. The passing of the frontier and the peaceful outcome of the bitter conflict between capital and labor had removed two of the major sources of American violence. The last assassination of a President had occurred in 1901 (in contrast to the 37-year period from 1865 to 1901 when three Presidents were slain), and that chapter of American violence seemed to have ended. The trend toward integration of the races and the absence of race riots and lynchings in the post-World War II years seemed to bode the end of a fourth kind of violence, racial antagonism.

In retrospect we now see that beneath the calm of the violence-free 1940s and 1950s there smoldered the urban and racial tensions and conflicts of generations that have erupted furiously in recent years. Chastened by the outburst of violence in the last decade, we now perceive that violence is a much more basic American problem than we had thought. For the first time in our history we realize that violence may be our national nemesis. This awareness may be the most hopeful sign of all, for the solution of any problem begins with self-knowledge.

The following collection of documents aims to present a true spectrum of American violence. Urban violence in its many forms is represented in 15 selections; racial conflict in 8; ethnic and labor violence in 8; and vigilantism and lynching in 9. Agrarian uprisings are represented by two of the largest and most typical—the New York anti-rent movement and the Kentucky Night Riders. A number of other cases—Nat Turner's Rebellion, *the South Carolina Regulators,* and the White Caps—illustrate the generally violent nature of rural America. The brutal war between whites and Indians is treated twice. The three most recent presidential assassins are depicted. There are single selections on the Western gunman, the family feud, the mass murderer, organized crime, and excessive violence in the enforcement of the law. The riot as a form of violence is represented at least 10 times. The internal violence associated with American wars is considered in 2 selections, dealing with the coming of the American Revolution and anti-draft activity in the Civil War.

In the last decade four major presidential commissions have focused on violence: the President's Commission on the Assassination of President Kennedy (Warren Commission), the President's Commission on Law Enforcement and the Administration of Justice (Katzenbach Commission), The National Advisory Commission on Civil Disorders (Kerner Commission), and the National Commission on the Causes and Prevention of Violence (Eisenhower Commission). All four of these commissions are represented in this volume. Included also is an excerpt from a report of an earlier presidential commission: the National Commission on Law Observance and Enforcement (Wickersham Commission, 1931).

I

PROLOGUE

1 / Abraham Lincoln on the Challenge of Violence to the Perpetuation of Our Political Institutions, 1837

One of the earliest and best statements on the problem of American violence was that made by youthful Abraham Lincoln at the age of 27 before the Springfield, Illinois, Lyceum on January 27, 1837. The 1830s were a decade of notable turbulence. With urban riots rending the East and lynchings plaguing the South and the West, Lincoln realized that the very foundations of American government were threatened. That Lincoln's address is still so timely is a measure not only of his penetrating insight but also of how little progress we have made since 1837.[1]

As a subject for the remarks of the evening, "The perpetuation of our political institutions" is selected.

In the great journal of things happening under the sun, we, the American people, find our account running under date of the nineteenth century of the Christian era. We find ourselves in the peaceful possession of the fairest portion of the earth as regards extent of territory, fertility of soil, and salubrity of climate. We find ourselves under the government of a system of political institutions conducing more essentially to the ends of civil and religious liberty than any of which the history of former times tells us. We, when mounting the stage of

From *John G. Nicolay* and *John Hay*, eds., Complete Works of Abraham Lincoln, *revised edition* (New York: Lamb Publishing Company, 1905), I, 35–42.

[1] In the documents that follow, ellipses indicate deletions from the text. In certain cases, modern principles of paragraphing have been adopted. Some of the selections contained footnotes in their original form. The footnotes have been omitted in order to conserve space.

existence, found ourselves the legal inheritors of these fundamental blessings. We toiled not in the acquirement or establishment of them; they are a legacy bequeathed us by a once hardy, brave, and patriotic, but now lamented and departed, race of ancestors. Theirs was the task (and nobly they performed it) to possess themselves, and through themselves us, of this goodly land, and to uprear upon its hills and its valleys a political edifice of liberty and equal rights; 'tis ours only to transmit these—the former unprofaned by the foot of an invader, the latter undecayed by the lapse of time and untorn by usurpation—to the latest generation that fate shall permit the world to know. This task of gratitude to our fathers, justice to ourselves, duty to posterity, and love for our species in general, all imperatively require us faithfully to perform.

How then shall we perform it? At what point shall we expect the approach of danger? By what means shall we fortify against it? Shall we expect some transatlantic military giant to step the ocean and crush us at a blow? Never! All the armies of Europe, Asia, and Africa combined, with all the treasure of the earth (our own excepted) in their military chest, with a Bonaparte for a commander, could not by force take a drink from the Ohio or make a track on the Blue Ridge in a trial of a thousand years.

At what point, then, is the approach of danger to be expected? I answer, If it ever reach us it must spring up amongst us; it cannot come from abroad. If destruction be our lot we must ourselves be its author and finisher. As a nation of freemen we must live through all time, or die by suicide.

I hope I am over wary; but if I am not, there is even now something of ill omen amongst us. I mean the increasing disregard for law which pervades the country—the growing disposition to substitute the wild and furious passions in lieu of the sober judgment of courts, and the worse than savage mobs for the executive ministers of justice. This disposition is awfully fearful in any community; and that it now exists in ours, though grating to our feelings to admit, it would be a violation of truth and an insult to our intelligence to deny. Accounts of outrages committed by mobs form the every-day news of the times. They have pervaded the country from New England to Louisiana; they are neither peculiar to the eternal snows of the former nor the burning suns of the latter; they are not the creature of climate, neither are they confined to the slaveholding or the non-slaveholding States. Alike they spring up among the pleasure-hunting masters of Southern slaves, and the order-loving citizens of the land of steady habits. Whatever then their cause may be, it is common to the whole country.

It would be tedious as well as useless to recount the horrors of all of them. Those happening in the State of Mississippi and at St. Louis are perhaps the most dangerous in example and revolting to humanity. In the Mississippi case they first commenced by hanging the regular gamblers—a set of men certainly not following for a livelihood a very useful or very honest occupation, but one which, so far from being forbidden by the laws, was actually licensed by an act of the Legislature passed but a single year before. Next, negroes suspected of conspiring to raise an insurrection were caught up and hanged in all parts of the State; then, white men supposed to be leagued with the negroes; and finally, strangers from neighboring States, going thither on business, were in many instances subjected to the same fate. Thus went on this process of hanging, from gamblers to negroes, from negroes to white citizens, and from these to strangers, till dead men were seen literally dangling from the boughs of trees upon every road-side, and in numbers almost sufficient to rival the native Spanish moss of the country as a drapery of the forest.

Turn, then, to that horror-striking scene at St. Louis. A single victim only was sacrificed there. This story is very short, and is perhaps the most highly tragic of anything of its length that has ever been witnessed in real life. A mulatto man by the name of McIntosh was seized in the street, dragged to the suburbs of the city, chained to a tree, and actually burned to death; and all within a single hour from the time he had been a freeman attending to his own business and at peace with the world.

Such are the effects of mob law, and such are the scenes becoming more and more frequent in this land so lately famed for love of law and order, and the stories of which have even now grown too familiar to attract anything more than an idle remark.

But you are perhaps ready to ask, "What has this to do with the perpetuation of our political institutions?" I answer, "It has much to do with it." Its direct consequences are, comparatively speaking, but a small evil, and much of its danger consists in the proneness of our minds to regard its direct as its only consequences. Abstractly considered, the hanging of the gamblers at Vicksburg was of but little consequence. They constitute a portion of population that is worse than useless in any community; and their death, if no pernicious example be set by it, is never matter of reasonable regret with any one. If they were annually swept from the stage of existence by the plague or smallpox, honest men would perhaps be much profited by the operation. Similar, too, is the correct reasoning in regard to the burning of the negro at St. Louis. He had forfeited his life by the perpetration of an outrageous murder upon one of the most worthy and respectable citizens of the city, and had he not died as he did, he must have died by the sentence of the law in a very short time afterward. As to him alone, it was as well the way it was as it could otherwise have been. But the example in either case was fearful. When men take it in their heads to-day to hang gamblers or burn murderers, they should recollect that in the confusion usually attending such transactions they will be as likely to hang or burn some one who is neither a gambler nor a murderer as one who is, and that, acting upon the example they set, the mob of to-morrow may, and probably will, hang or burn some of them by the very same mistake. And not only so; the innocent, those who have ever set their faces against violations of law in every shape, alike with the guilty fall victims to the ravages of mob law; and thus it goes up, step by step, till all the walls erected for the defense of the persons and property of individuals are trodden down and disregarded. But all this, even, is not the full extent of the evil. By such examples, by instances of the perpetrators of such acts going unpunished, the lawless in spirit are encouraged to become lawless in practice; and having been used to no restraint but dread of punishment, they thus become absolutely unrestrained. Having ever regarded government as their deadliest bane, they make a jubilee of the suspension of its operations, and pray for nothing so much as its total annihilation. While, on the other hand, good men, men who love tranquillity, who desire to abide by the laws and enjoy their benefits, who would gladly spill their blood in the defense of their country, seeing their property destroyed, their families insulted, and their lives endangered, their persons injured, and seeing nothing in prospect that forebode a change for the better, become tired of and disgusted with a government that offers them no protection, and are not much averse to a change in which they imagine they have nothing to lose. Thus, then, by the operation of this mobocratic spirit which all must admit is now abroad in the land, the strongest bulwark of any government, and particularly of those constituted like ours, may effectually be broken down and destroyed—I mean the attachment of the people. Whenever this effect shall be produced among us; whenever the vicious portion of population shall be permitted to gather bands of hundreds and thousands, and burn churches, ravage and rob provision-stores, throw printing-presses into rivers, shoot editors, and hang and burn obnoxious persons at pleasure and with impunity, depend on it, this government cannot last. By such things the feelings of the best citizens will become more or less alienated from it, and thus it will be left without friends, or with too few, and those few too weak to make their friendship effectual. At such a time, and under such circumstances, men of sufficient talent and ambition will not be wanting to seize the opportunity, strike the blow, and overturn that fair fabric which for the last half century has been the fondest hope of the lovers of freedom throughout the world.

II

VIOLENCE IN THE SEVENTEENTH AND EIGHTEENTH CENTURIES

2 / "The Late Revolution in New England," April 18, 1689

The late sevententh century was a turbulent period in American history. Among the upheavals were Bacon's Rebellion in Virginia (1676), Culpeper's Rebellion in North Carolina (1678), Leisler's Rebellion in New York (1689), and Coode's Rebellion in Maryland (1689). The last two paralleled the overthrow of James II in England (1689) and, along with the uprising against Governor Edmund Andros in Boston, constituted the "Glorious Revolution in America." As governor of the Dominion of New England, Andros ruled a vast domain. The main resistance to his autocratic ways developed in Massachusetts where his arbitrary attack on local government and land titles angered many. Protestant Bostonians also feared (unjustly) that he was secretly a Roman Catholic in league with the French enemy. The following account by Nathanael Byfield describes the mass rebellion that toppled Andros and his regime.

I am willing to give you some brief Account of the most remarkable things that have happened here within this Fortnight last past. . . .

Upon the *Eighteenth* Instant, about Eight of the Clock in the Morning, in *Boston*, it was reported at the *South* end of the Town, That at the *North* end they were all in Arms; and the like Report was at the *North* end, respecting the *South* end: Whereupon Captain *John George*

From the pamphlet by Nathanael Byfield, An Account of the Late Revolution in New England (*London: Ric. Chiswell, 1689*), *reprinted in Peter Force, ed.*, Tracts and Other Papers Relating Principally to the . . . Colonies in North America . . . , *4 vols.* (*Washington: Peter Force, 1836–46*), *Vol. IV, Tract No. 10.*

was immediately seized, and about nine of the clock the Drums beat thorough the Town; and an Ensign was set up upon the Beacon. Then Mr. *Bradstreet,* Mr. *Danforth,* Major *Richards,* Dr. *Cooke,* and Mr. *Addington &c.* were brought to the Council-house by a Company of Soldiers under the Command of Captain *Hill.* The mean while the People in Arms, did take up and put in to Goal, Justice *Bullivant,* Justice *Foxcroft,* Mr. *Randolf,* Sheriff *Sherlock,* Captain *Ravenscroft,* Captain *White, Farewel, Broadbent, Crafford, Larkin, Smith,* and many more, as also *Mercey* the then Goal-keeper, and put *Scates* the Bricklayer in his place.

About Noon, in the Gallery at the Council-house, was read the Declaration here inclosed.[1] Then a Message was sent to the Fort to Sir *Edmund Andros,* By Mr. *Oliver* and Mr. *Eyres,* signed by the Gentlemen then in the Council-Chamber, (which is here also inclosed); to inform him how unsafe he was like to be if he did not deliver up himself, and Fort and Government forthwith, which he was loath to do. By this time, being about two of the Clock (the Lecture being put by) the Town was generally in Arms, and so many of the Countrey came in, that there was Twenty Companies in *Boston,* besides a great many that appeared at *Charles Town* that could not get over (some say Fifteen Hundred).

There then came information to the Soldiers, That a Boat was come from the Frigat that made towards the Fort, which made them haste thither, and come to the Sconce soon after the Boat got thither; and 'tis said that Governor *Andros,* and about half a score Gentlemen, were coming down out of the Fort; but the Boat being seized, wherein were small Arms, Hand-Granadoes, and a quantity of Match, the Governour and the rest went in again; whereupon Mr. *John Nelson,* who was at the head of the Soldiers, did demand the Fort and the Governor, who was loath to submit to them; but at length did come down, and was with the Gentlemen that were with him, conveyed to the Council-house, where Mr. *Bradstreet* and the rest of the Gentlemen waited to receive him; to whom Mr. *Stoughton* first spake, telling him, He might thank himself for the present disaster that had befallen him, *&c.* He was then confined for that night to Mr. *John Usher's* house under strong Guards, and the next day conveyed to the Fort, (where he yet remains, and with him Lieutenant Collonel *Ledget*) which is under the Command of Mr. *John Nelson;* and at the Castle,

---

[1] [*The Declaration attacked Andros for his arbitrary and oppressive rule; his attack on land titles and local government were among the many grievances cited against him. The Message to him was a firm request that he surrender peacefully.*]

which is under the Command of Mr. *John Fairweather,* is Mr. *West,*
Mr. *Graham,* Mr. *Palmer,* and Captaine *Tryfroye.*

At that time Mr. *Dudley* was out upon the Circuit, and was holding
a Court at *Southold* on *Long-Island.* And on the 21*st.* Instant he arrived
at *Newport,* where he heard the News. The next day Letters came to
him, advising him not to come home; he thereupon went over privately to Major *Smith's* at *Naraganzett,* and advice is this day come
hither, that yesterday about a dozen young men, most of their own
heads, went thither to demand him; and are gone with him down to
Boston. We have also advice, that on *Fryday* last towards evening,
Sir *Edmond Andros* did attempt to make an escape in Womans Ap-
parel, and pass'd two Guards, and was stopped at the third, being
discovered by his Shoes, not having changed them.

3 / The New York City Slave Uprising of 1712

*The urban racial violence that has had such a tremendous impact
on America in the 1960s goes far back into the country's past. As early
as 1712 New York City had a slave uprising that failed. In 1741 there
was another abortive slave uprising in New York City (and also in
Newark, New Jersey), which was put down with great severity and
in which sixteen blacks and three whites were killed. The account
of the 1712 uprising that follows is from a letter of Governor Robert
Hunter of New York to the British Board of Trade on June 23, 1712.*

I must now give your Lordships an account of a bloody conspiracy
of some of the slaves of this place, to destroy as many of the Inhabitants as they could. It was put in execution in this manner, when they
had resolved to revenge themselves, for some hard usage they apprehended to have received from their masters (for I can find no other
cause) they agreed to meet in the orchard of Mr. Crook the middle
of the Town, some provided with fire arms, some with swords and
others with knives and hatchets[;] this was the sixth day of April,
the time of meeting was about twelve or one o'clock in the night, when
about three and twenty of them were got togeather[;] one coffee and
negroe slave to one Vantilburgh set fire to an out house of his Masters,
and then repairing to the place where the rest were they all sallyed
out togeather with their arm's and marched to the fire[;] by this time

From E. B. O'Callaghan, ed., Documents Relative to the Colonial History of
the State of New York . . . *(Albany: Weed, Parsons & Co., 1855), V, 341.*

the noise of fire spreeding through the town, the people began to flock to it[;] upon the approach of severall the slaves fired and killed them, the noise of the guns gave the allarm, and some escaping their shot soon published the cause of the fire, which was the reason, that not above nine Christians were killed, and about five or six wounded[;] upon the first notice which was very soon after the mischeif was begun, I order'd a detachment from the fort under a proper officer to march against them, but the slaves made their retreat into the woods, by the favour of the night[;] having ordered centries the next day in the most proper places on the Island to prevent their escape, I caused the day following the Militia of this town and of the county of west Chester to drive the Island, and by this means and strict searches in the town, we found all that put the design in execution, six of these having first laid violent hands upon themselves, the rest were forthwith brought to their tryal before ye Justices of this place who are authorized by Act of Assembly, to hold a Court in such cases. In that Court were twenty seven condemned whereof twenty one were executed, one being a woman with child, her execution by that meanes suspended [;] some were burnt others hanged, one broke on the wheele, and one hung a live in chains in the town, so that there has been the most exemplary punishment inflicted that could be possibly thought of.

4 / Urban Violence in the Colonial Period:
The Boston Impressment Riot of 1747

America's earliest cities—the bustling colonial ports of Boston, Newport, New York, Philadelphia, and Charleston—had their share of violence, contributed in large part by the tumultuous lower-class population connected with the maritime industry: seamen, dock workers, laborers, artisans, and so forth. On November 17, 1747, this element of the Boston population ("armed seamen, servants, Negroes and others") rioted against an attempt to impress local men for service in the Royal Navy. For three days the rioters dominated the city, and the governor was forced to flee to the "castle" on an island in the bay. The freeing of most of the impressed men amounted to a substantial victory for the rioters. Mob action by this segment of the

Modernized from Thomas Hutchinson, The History of the Province of Massachusetts-Bay . . . 1691–1750 (*Boston: Thomas and John Fleet, 1767*), pp. 330–33.

urban population in the 1760s and 1770s helped to bring on the American Revolution.

In 1747 (Nov. 17th) happened a tumult in the town of Boston equal to any which had preceded it, although far short of some that have happened since. Mr. Knowles was commodore of a number of men of war then in the harbour of Nantasket. Some of the sailors had deserted. The commodore . . . thought it reasonable that Boston should supply him with as many men as he had lost and, sent his boats up to town early in the morning, and surprized not only as many seamen as could be found on board any of the ships, outward bound as well as others, but swept the wharfs also, taking some ship carpenters apprentices and labouring land men. However tolerable such a surprize might have been in London it could not be borne here. The people had not been used to it and men of all orders resented it, but the lower class were beyond measure enraged and soon assembled with sticks, clubs, pitchmops, &c. They first seized an innocent lieutenant who happened to be ashore upon other business. They had then formed no scheme, and the speaker of the house passing by and assuring them that he knew that the lieutenant had no hand in the press they suffered him to be led off to a place of safety. The mob increasing and having received intelligence that several of the commanders were at the governor's house, it was agreed to go and demand satisfaction. The house was soon surrounded and the court, or yard before the house, filled, but many persons of discretion inserted themselves and prevailed so far as to prevent the mob from entering. Several of the officers had planted themselves at the head of the stair way with loaded carbines and seemed determined to preserve their liberty or lose their lives. A deputy sheriff attempting to exercise his authority, was seized by the mob and carried away in triumph and set in the stocks, which afforded them diversion and tended to abate their rage and disposed them to separate and go to dinner.

As soon as it was dusk, several thousand people assembled in king-street, below the town house where the general court was sitting. Stones and brickbatts were thrown through the glass into the council chamber. The governor, however, with several gentlemen of the council and house ventured into the balcony and, after silence was obtained, the governor in a well judged speech expressed his great disapprobation of the impress and promised his utmost endeavours to obtain the discharge of every one of the inhabitants, and at the same time gently reproved the irregular proceedings both of the forenoon and evening. Other gentlemen also attempted to persuade the people to disperse and wait to see what steps the general court would take. All was to no purpose. The seizure and restraint of the commanders and other officers who were in town was insisted upon as the only effectual method to procure the release of the inhabitants aboard the ships.

It was thought adviseable for the governor to withdraw to his house, many of the officers of the militia and other gentlemen attending him. A report was raised that a barge from one of the ships was come to a wharf in the town. The mob flew to seize it, but by mistake took a boat belonging to a Scotch ship and dragged it, with as much seeming ease through the streets as if it had been in the water, to the governor's house and prepared to burn it before the house, but from a consideration of the danger of setting the town on fire were diverted and the boat was burnt in a place of less hazard. The next day the governor ordered that the military officers of Boston should cause their companies to be mustered and to appear in arms, and that a military watch should be kept the succeeding night, but the drummers were interrupted and the militia refused to appear. The governor did not think it for his honour to remain in town another night and privately withdrew to the castle. A number of gentlemen who had some intimation of his design, sent a message to him by Col. Hutchinson, assuring him they would stand by him in maintaining the authority of government and restoring peace and order, but he did not think this sufficient.

The governor wrote to Mr. Knowles representing the confusions occasioned by this extravagant act of his officers, but he refused all terms of accommodation until the commanders and other officers on shore were suffered to go on board their ships, and he threatened to bring up his ships and bombard the town, and some of them coming to sail, caused different conjectures of his real intention. Capt. Erskine of the Canterbury had been seized at the house of Col. Brinley in Roxbury and given his parole not to go abroad, and divers inferior officers had been secured.

The 17th, 18th and part of the 19th, the council and house of representatives, sitting in the town, went on with their ordinary business, not willing to interpose lest they should encourage other commanders of the navy to future acts of the like nature, but towards noon of the 19th some of the principal members of the house began to think more seriously of the dangerous consequence of leaving the governor without support when there was not the least ground of exception to his conduct. Some high spirits in the town began to question whether his retiring should be deemed a desertion or abdication. It was moved to appoint a committee of the two houses to consider what was proper to be done. This would take time and was excepted to, and the speaker was desired to draw up such resolves as it was thought necessary the house should immediately agree to, and they were passed by a considerable majority and made public.

In the house of representatives, Nov. 19th, 1747.

Resolved, that there has been and still continues, a tumultuous riotous assembling of armed seamen, servants, negroes and others in the town of Boston, tending to the destruction of all government and order.

Resolved, that it is incumbent on the civil and military officers in the province to exert themselves to the utmost, to discourage and suppress all such tumultuous riotous proceedings whensoever they may happen.

Resolved, that this house will stand by and support with their lives and estates his excellency the governor and the executive part of the government in all endeavors for this purpose.

Resolved, that this house will exert themselves by all ways and means possible in redressing such grievances as his majesty's subjects are and have been under, which may have been the cause of the aforesaid tumultuous disorderly assembling together.

T. Hutchinson, Speaker.

The council passed a vote ordering that Captain Erskine and all other officers belonging to his majesty's ships should be forthwith set at liberty and protected by the government, which was concurred by the house. As soon as these votes were known, the tumultuous spirit began to subside. The inhabitants of the town of Boston assembled in town meeting in the afternoon, having been notified to consider, in general, what was proper for them to do upon this occasion, and notwithstanding it was urged by many that all measures to suppress the present spirit in the people would tend to encourage the like oppressive acts for the future, yet the contrary party prevailed and the town, although they expressed their sense of the great insult and injury by the impress, condemned the tumultuous riotous acts of such as had insulted the governor and the other branches of the legislature and committed many other heinous offences.

The governor, not expecting so favorable a turn, had wrote to the secretary to prepare orders for the colonels of the regiments of Cambridge, Roxbury and Milton and the regiment of horse to have their officers and men ready to march at an hour's warning to such place of rendezvous as he should direct, but the next day there was an uncommon appearance of the militia of the town of Boston, many persons taking their muskets who never carried one upon any other occasion, and the governor was conducted to his house with as great parade as when he first assumed the government.

The commodore dismissed most, if not all, of the inhabitants who had been impressed, and the squadron sailed to the joy of the rest of the town.

5 / The Origins of American Vigilantism:
Regulators and Lynch-Law, 1767–80

Vigilantism is often thought of as a feature of the western plains and mountains, but the roots of American vigilantism actually reach back to the South Carolina and Virginia Piedmont in the late colonial and Revolutionary period. The South Carolina regulator movement of 1767–69 was the first vigilante movement in American history. Although now an obsolete term, "regulator" was the term used to denote the vigilante in the eighteenth and early nineteenth centuries. "Vigilance committee" and "vigilante" did not come into vogue until the middle of the nineteenth century. Lacking county courts and sheriffs, the regulators of the South Carolina back country took the law into their own hands while demanding the establishment of their own system of justice. Their movement was successful in every way. Related to the regulator movement was the development of lynch-law in the Piedmont of Virginia in 1780. Both the regulator spirit and lynch-law were taken across the Appalachian Mountains by the pioneers after the Revolutionary War.

The Plan of Regulation in South Carolina, 1768

Extract of a Letter from a Gentleman at Peede, to his Friend in [Charleston].

I wish you would inform me what is generally thought in town of the *Regulators,* who now reign uncontrolled in all the remote parts of the province. In June, they held a Congress at the Congarees,

From the South-Carolina and American General Gazette (*Charleston, South Carolina*), September 2, 1768.

where a vast number of people assembled, several of the principal settlers on the river, men of property, among the rest. When these returned, they requested the most respectable people in these parts to meet on a certain day; they did so, and upon the report made to them, they unanimously adopted the *Plan of Regulation,* and are now executing it with indefatigable ardour.

Their regulation is, in general, effectually to deny the jurisdiction of the courts holden in Charleston over those parts of the province that ought to be by rights out of it; to purge, by measures of their own, the country of all idle persons, all that have not a visible way of getting an honest living, all that are suspected or known to be guilty of mal-practices; and also to prevent the service of any writ or warrant from Charlestown; so that a deputy-marshal would be handled by them with severity, against these they breathe high indignation.—They are every day, excepting sundays [*sic*], employed in this *Regulation Work* as they term it. They have brought many under the lash and are scourging and banishing the baser sort of people, such as above, with unwearied diligence. Such as they think reclaimable they are a little tender of; and these they task, giving them so many acres to attend in so many days, on pain of Flagellation, that they may not be reduced to poverty, and by that be led to steal from their industrious neighbours. This course, they say, they are determined to pursue, with every other effectual measure that will answer their purpose; and that they will defend themselves in it to the last extremity.

Lynch-Law in Virginia, 1780

The movement for independence had from the first a great many opponents in the mountainous sections of Virginia, and there was a considerable number of Tories in Bedford County, where Charles Lynch lived. The unsettled condition of affairs also led many desperadoes to resort to this section of Virginia. Both Tories and desperadoes harassed the Continentals and plundered their property with impunity. The prices paid by both armies for horses made horse-stealing a lucrative practice, and the inefficiency of the judiciary made punishment practically out of the question. The county courts were merely examining courts in all such cases, and the single court

From *James E. Cutler*, Lynch-Law . . . (*New York: Longmans, Green, 1905*), pp. 24–30.

for the final trial of felonies sat at Williamsburg, more than two hundred miles away. To take the prisoners thither, and the witnesses necessary to convict them, was next to impossible. Frequently the officers in charge of prisoners would be attacked by outlaws and forced to release their men, or be captured by British troops and themselves made prisoners.

It was under these circumstances that Colonel Lynch conferred with some of his neighbors as to what was best to be done. After deliberation they decided to take matters into their own hands, to punish lawlessness of every kind, and so far as possible restore peace and security to their community. For the purpose of attaining these ends they formed an organization with Mr. Lynch at the head. Under his direction suspected persons were arrested and brought to his house, where they were tried by a court composed of himself, as presiding justice, and his three neighbors, William Preston, Robert Adams, Jr., and James Callaway, sitting as associate justices.

The practice of this court was to have the accused brought face to face with his accusers, permit him to hear the testimony against himself, and to allow him to defend himself by calling witnesses in his behalf and by showing mitigating and extenuating circumstances. If aquitted, he was allowed to go, "often with apologies and reparation." If convicted, he was sentenced to receive thirty-nine lashes on the bare back, and if he did not then shout "Liberty Forever," to be hanged up by the thumbs until he did so. The execution of the sentence took place immediately upon conviction. The condemned was tied to a large walnut tree standing in Mr. Lynch's yard and the stripes inflicted—with such vigor, it is said, that even the stoutest hearted Tory shouted for "Liberty" without necessitating a resort to further punishment. . . .

The proceedings in Bedford, which the legislature pronounced to be illegal, but justifiable, were imitated in other parts of the State, and came to be known by the name of Lynch's Law. In justice to Colonel Lynch, it should be remembered that his action was taken at a time when the State was in the throes of a hostile invasion. The General Court, before which the conspirators should have been tried, was temporarily dispersed. Thomas Jefferson, then the governor of the State, was proving himself peculiarly incompetent to fill the position. The whole executive department was in a state of partial paralysis. It was, therefore, no spirit of insubordination or disregard of the law that induced Lynch to act as he did. There were few men living more inclined than this simple Quaker farmer to render due respect in word and deed to the established authorities.

A Regulator Whipping with Fiddle-Playing, 1769

Typical of the punishments of the Virginia lynch-law movement and later frontier vigilantes was the whipping inflicted on one John Harvey by South Carolina regulators in 1769. The orgiastic character that such whippings often had is revealed by the playing of a fiddle and the beating of a drum during Harvey's ordeal. The following account is from a court action brought by Harvey against the leader of the regulator band, Robinson.

. . . in the month of September in the year 1769 The plaintiff Harvey was Seized by a large body of people amounting in number to about fifty or sixty, among whom the Defendant Robinson was who appeared to be the Captain or leader of the party that at a place called Nobles Creek, they chained the plaintiff Harvey with a Waggon Chain and locked to a Sapling or young tree, that they Stripped him to his Shirt & after keeping him Chained in that manner for about two hours, they whipped him alternately for the Space of an hour with Bundles of rods or Switches each person giving him Ten Stripes, until he had received in the whole five hundred Stripes, that Robinson gave him Ten Stripes in his turn & that the blood Streamed down his back & from the account of one of the Witnesses who saw him Some days after it appeared that his Back was then in a Shocking Condition very sore & much festered[,] that one of the witnesses, before Harvey was whipped was invited by the mob to Join with them, that he refused to do so & told them it was inhumane in them to use their fellow Creatures in that manner, that he asked why they whipped him and they answered because he was roguish & troublesome, & on being asked how they did prove him to be So, they answered they would not be at the trouble; that the mob had during this whole transaction a drum beating and a fiddle playing.

From *South Carolina Council Journal*, February 3, 1772 (*manuscript in South Carolina Archives, Columbia*).

6 / Violence Brings on the American Revolution, 1765–73

Boston Riots Against the Stamp Act

To a considerable extent the American Revolution may be viewed as a decade-long wave of urban rioting and upheaval that evolved into open rebellion. The first major outbreak of urban violence in resistance to British policy was the rioting that greeted the first move toward enforcement of the Stamp Act. Violent opposition to the Stamp Act was led in Boston and elsewhere by the Sons of Liberty, who were generally middle-class professionals, artisans, and tradesmen. Dominating the riotous mobs were lower-class seamen, dockers, and workers. Hence violent resistance to British policy before the Revolution entailed a combination of middle-class leadership and lower-class deeds. In regard to the Stamp Act, violence was directed mainly against those who had been (or were expected to be) designated as stamp distributors and against those suspected of supporting the Stamp Act. In the colonies as a whole, violence or the threat of violence prevented the Stamp Act from being enforced—even before Parliament repealed it.

In the account below Andrew Oliver was the prospective stamp distributor, Francis Bernard was the Royal Governor, Thomas Hutchinson was the Lieutenant-Governor and Chief Justice, and Jonathan Mayhew was a leading patriotic clergyman.

The daybreak of Wednesday, the fourteenth of August, saw the effigy of Oliver tricked out with emblems of Bute and Grenville, swinging on the bough of a stately elm, the pride of the neighborhood, known as the Great Tree, standing near what was then the entrance to the town. The pageant had been secretly prepared by Boston mechanics, true-born Sons of Liberty, Benjamin Edes, the printer, Thomas Crafts, the painter; John Smith and Stephen Cleverly, the braziers; and the younger Avery; Thomas Chase, a fiery hater of kings; Henry Bass, and Henry Welles. The passers-by stopped to gaze on

From *George Bancroft*, History of the United States . . . (*Boston: Little, Brown and Company, 1860*), V, 310–13.

the grotesque spectacle, and their report collected thousands. Hutchinson, as chief justice, ordered the sheriff to remove the image. "We will take them down ourselves at evening," said the people.

Bernard summoned his council. "The country, whatever may be the consequence," said some of them, "will never submit to the execution of the Stamp Act." The majority spoke against interfering with the people. The day passed, and evening came, and Bernard and Hutchinson were still engaged in impotent altercations with their advisers, when, just after dark, an "amazing" multitude, moving in the greatest order and following the images borne on a bier, after passing down the main street, marched directly through the old State House and under the council-chamber itself, shouting at the top of their voices: "Liberty, Property, and no Stamps." Giving three huzzas of defiance, they next, in Kilby-street, demolished a frame which they thought Oliver was building for a Stamp-Office, and with the wooden trophies made a funeral pyre for his effigy in front of his house on Fort Hill.

"The Stamp Act shall not be executed here," exclaimed one who spoke the general sentiment. "Death to the man who offers a piece of stamped paper to sell!" cried others. "All the power of Great Britain," said a third, "shall not oblige us to submit to the Stamp Act." "We will die," declared even the sober-minded, "we will die upon the place first." "We have sixty thousand fighting-men in this colony alone," wrote Mayhew. "And we will spend our last blood in the cause," repeated his townsmen.

Hutchinson directed the colonel of the militia to beat an alarm. "My drummers," said he, "are in the mob." With the sheriff, Hutchinson went up to disperse the crowd. "Stand by, my boys," cried a ringleader; "let no man give way"; and Hutchinson, as he fled, was obliged to run the gauntlet, yet escaping with one or two blows. At eleven, the multitude repaired to the Province House, where Bernard lived, and after three cheers, they dispersed quietly.

"We have a dismal prospect before us," said Hutchinson, the next morning, anticipating tragical events in some of the colonies. "The people of Connecticut," reported one whose name is not given, "have threatened to hang their distributor on the first tree after he enters the colony." "If Oliver," said Bernard, with rueful gravity, "had been found last night, he would certainly have been murthered." "If he does not resign," thought many, "there will be another riot to-night, and his house will be pulled down about his ears." So the considerate self-seeker, with the bitterness of enduring anger and disappointed avarice in his heart, seasonably in the day-time, "gave it under his own hand," that he would not serve as Stamp Officer, while Bernard, deserting his post as guardian of the public peace, hurried trembling to the castle, and could not recover from his fears, though immured within the walls of a fortress. At night, a bonfire on Fort Hill celebrated the people's victory. Several hundred men were likewise gathered round the house of Hutchinson. "Let us but hear from his own mouth," said their leader, "that he is not in favor of the Stamp Act, and we will be easy." But Hutchinson evaded a reply.

The governor, just before his retreat, ordered a proclamation for the discovery and arrest of the rioters. "If discovery were made," said Hutchinson, "it would not be possible to commit them." "The prisons," said Mayhew, "would not hold them many hours. In this town, and within twenty miles of it, ten thousand men would soon be collected together on such an occasion." And on the next Lord's Day but one, before a crowded audience, choosing as his text,—"I would they were even cut off which trouble you; for, brethren, ye have been called unto liberty,"—he preached fervidly in behalf of civil and religious freedom. "I hope," said he, "no persons among ourselves have encouraged the bringing such a burden as the Stamp Act on the country."

The distrust of the people fell more and more upon Hutchinson.— "He is a prerogative man," they cried. "He grasps at all the important offices in the state."—"He himself holds four, and his relations six or seven more."—"He wiped out of the petition of Massachusetts every spirited expression."—"He prevailed to get a friend of Grenville made agent for the colony."—"He had a principal hand in projecting the Stamp Act."—"He advised Oliver against resigning."—"To enforce the acts of trade, he granted writs of assistance, which are no better than general warrants."—"He took depositions against the merchants as smugglers."

Thus the rougher spirits wrought one another into a frenzy. On the twenty-sixth of August, a bonfire in front of the Old State House collected at nightfall a mixed crowd. They first burned all the records of the hated Vice-Admiralty Court; they next ravaged the house of the Comptroller of the Customs; and then, giving Hutchinson and his family barely time to escape, split open his doors with broadaxes, broke his furniture, scattered his plate and ready money, his books and manuscripts, and at daybreak left his house a ruin.

The coming morning, the citizens of Boston, in town-meeting, expressed their "detestation of these violent proceedings," and pledged themselves to one another to "suppress the like disorders for the future." "I had rather lose my hand," said Mayhew, "than encourage such outrages"; and Samuel Adams agreed with him; but they, and nearly all the townsmen, and the whole continent, applauded the proceedings of the fourteenth of August; and the elm, beneath which the people had on that day assembled, was solemnly named "the Tree of Liberty."

The Tarring and Feathering of a British Henchman, 1769

The final violent phase in the relations between the mother country and the colonies continued with three crucial events in the early 1770s. First occurred the "Boston Massacre" in March 1770; next came the burning of the royal schooner Gaspee *by Rhode Islanders in June 1772; and, finally, the "Boston Tea Party" of December 1773—the incident that set off a chain reaction leading directly to the Declaration of Independence. At the same time American patriots increased their coercive actions against British sympathizers—opprobriously termed "Tories" in the 1770s. It was in this period that the American folk punishment of tarring and feathering was popularized; patriots used tar and feathers to punish and intimidate British sympathizers and henchmen as described in the Boston case below.*

Last Thursday afternoon a young Woman from the Country was decoyed into one of the [British] Barracks in Town, and most shamefully abused by some of the Soldiers there:—The Person that enticed her thither, with promises of disposing of all her marketing there (who also belonged to the Country), was afterwards taken by the Populace and several times duck'd in the Water at one of the Docks in Town; but luckily for him he made his escape from them sooner than intended:—however, we hear that after he crossed the Ferry to Charlestown, on his return home, the People there being informed of the base Part he had been acting, took him and placed him in a Cart, and after tarring and feathering him (the present popular Punishment for modern delinquents) they carried him about that Town for two or three Hours, as a Spectacle of Contempt and a Warning to others.

From the Boston Evening-Post, *November 6, 1769, p. 3.*

The Boston Massacre, March 5, 1770

The lower classes of Boston had been ever ready to riot against the British since the great impressment riot of 1747. During the winter of

From Frederic Kidder, History of the Boston Massacre . . . (*Albany: Joel Munsell, 1870*), *pp. 71–72.*

1769–70 feeling was especially high against the regular British troops stationed in Boston, whom local patriots accused of arrogance and brutality and with whom workingmen competed for jobs during the soldiers' off-duty hours. The tension came to a head on the night of Monday, March 5, 1770, when a detachment of the British regulars, harassed and goaded by inhabitants—especially boys in their teens or younger—fired on a mob and killed five and wounded others. Patriot agitators led by Samuel Adams scored the "Boston Massacre," as they called it, and used the event to stir up anti-British feeling. The five men killed were Samuel Gray, Patrick Carr, James Caldwell, Samuel Maverick, and Crispus Attucks, "an intrepid mulatto."

I, Thomas Cain, of lawful age, testify and say, that on Monday, the 5th instant, being in a house on the Long wharf, I heard a bell ring, which I imagined was for nine o'clock, but being informed by a person in my company that it was twelve minutes past that hour by his watch, I then concluded the bell rung for fire, so I ran up King street, in company with Mr. William Tant, and asking a few people whom I met the cause of the bell's ringing, was answered the soldiers had insulted some of the town's people by the ropewalks. I then went down Quaker lane as far as Justice Dana's house, where I met a number of people coming up, and asked them if there had been any disturbance at or near the ropewalks? They answered me, that there had been several people insulted and knocked down by the soldiers in different parts of the town. I then came up into King street, where they assembled together below the Town-house (to the best of my knowledge), between thirty and forty persons, mostly youngsters or boys, and when there they gave three cheers, and asked where the soldiers were (I imagine they meant them that had insulted them); some of the people assembled being near the sentry at the Custom-house door, damned him, and I saw some snow balls or other things throwed that way, whereupon the sentry stepped on the steps at the Custom-house door and loaded his piece, and when loaded struck the butt of his firelock against the steps three or four times, in the interim the people assembled, continuing crying, "Fire, fire, and be damned," and some of them drawing near to him he knocked at the Custom-house door very hard, whereupon the door was opened about half way, and I saw a person come out, which I imagined to be a servant without a hat, his hair tied and hung down loose.

In the space of about five minutes, to the best of my remembrance, I perceived a party of soldiers come from the main-guard directly through the concourse of people that was then in King street, with their muskets and fixed bayonets, pushing to and fro, saying, "Make way"; when they had got abreast of the Custom-house they drew up in a line from the corner of Royal Exchange lane to the sentry box at the Custom-house door, and being in that position for the space of five or six minutes, with their muskets levelled breast high and pointed at the people that was still in the street, huzzaing, &c., and crying fire, as before, and some more snowballs or other things being hove, I heard and saw the flash of a gun that went off near the corner of the afore-mentioned lane, and in the space of two seconds I heard the word "Fire" given, but by whom I cannot ascertain, but the soldiers fired regularly one after another, and when discharged, loaded again; I then stood behind the sentry box, between the soldier next it and the Custom-house.

Rhode Islanders Burn the *Gaspee*, June 10, 1772

Enforcement of customs regulations was a frequent source of friction between the colonists and the British in the 1760s and 1770s. In this period the British tightened their customs regulations in an attempt to halt the smuggling that had gone on almost continuously during the colonial period. Unfortunately, many British officials exceeded the regulations by overzealous and often illegal enforcement, which the historian Oliver M. Dickerson has described as "customs racketeering." Such an officer was Lieutenant Dudingston, commander of the British armed schooner Gaspee, *who had been harassing the farmers (who used small boats for short coastwise voyages) and seamen of Narragansett Bay since March 1772. When the* Gaspee *ran aground several miles south of Providence on June 10, 1772, a party was quickly formed to go out and burn the schooner. The group was led by John Brown, Rhode Island's leading merchant, and other prominent citizens. The following memoir is by participant Ephraim Bowen.*

About the time of the shutting up of the shops, soon after sunset, a man passed along the main street, beating a drum, and informing the inhabitants of the fact that the Gaspee was aground on Namquit Point, and would not float off until three o'clock, the next morning; and inviting those persons who felt a disposition to go and destroy that troublesome vessel, to repair in the evening to Mr. James Sabin's

From *John R. Bartlett,* A History of the Destruction of His Majesty's Schooner Gaspee . . . (*Providence: A. Crawford Greene, 1861*), *pp. 18–19.*

house. About nine o'clock, I took my father's gun, and my powder horn and bullets, and went to Mr. Sabin's, and found the south-east room full of people, where I loaded my gun, and all remained there till about ten o'clock, some casting bullets in the kitchen, and others making arrangements for departure, when orders were given to cross the street to Fenner's Wharf, and embark; which soon took place, and a sea captain acted as steersman of each boat; of whom, I recollect Capt. Abraham Whipple, Capt. John B. Hopkins (with whom I embarked), and Capt. Benjamin Dunn. A line, from right to left was soon formed, with Capt. Whipple on the right, and Capt. Hopkins on the right of the left wing.

The party thus proceeded, till within about sixty yards of the Gaspee, when a sentinel hailed, "Who comes there?" No answer. He hailed again, and no answer.

In about a minute, Dudingston mounted the starboard gunwale, in his shirt, and hailed, "Who comes there?" No answer. He hailed again, when Capt. Whipple answered as follows:

"I am the sheriff of the county of Kent, G—d d——n you. I have got a warrant to apprehend you, G—d d——n you; so surrender, G—d d——n you."

I took my seat on the main thwart, near the larboard row-lock, with my gun by my right side, facing forwards.

As soon as Dudingston began to hail, Joseph Bucklin, who was standing on the main thwart, by my right side, said to me, "Ephe, reach me your gun, and I can kill that fellow." I reached it to him, accordingly; when, during Capt. Whipple's replying, Bucklin fired, and Dudingston fell; and Bucklin exclaimed, "I have killed the rascal."

In less than a minute after Capt. Whipple's answer, the boats were alongside of the Gaspee, and boarded without opposition. The men on deck retreated below, as Dudingston entered the cabin.

As soon as it was discovered that he was wounded, John Mawney, who had for two or three years been studying physic and surgery, was ordered to go into the cabin, and dress Dudingston's wound, and I was directed to assist him. On examination, it was found the ball took effect about five inches directly below the navel. Dudingston called for Mr. Dickinson to produce bandages and other necessaries, for the dressing of the wound, and when finished, orders were given to the schooner's company to collect their clothing, and every thing belonging to them, and put them into their boats, as all of them were to be sent on shore.

All were soon collected, and put on board of the boats, including one of our boats. They departed, and landed Dudingston at the old

Still-house Wharf, at Pawtuxet, and put the chief into the house of Joseph Rhodes.

Soon after, all the party were ordered to depart, leaving one boat for the leaders of the expedition; who soon set the vessel on fire, which consumed her to the water's edge.

The Boston Tea Party, December 16, 1773

The Tea Act, passed by the British Parliament in 1773, enabled the East India Company to export tea directly to the American colonies. This had the effect of undercutting the established American tea merchants, who made plans to resist the act in New York, Philadelphia, Charleston, and Boston. Since mid-November 1773 the patriots and merchants of Boston had sought by negotiation to prevent the unloading of three tea ships tied up at Griffin's wharf. The negotiations failed, and leaders in the anti-British faction of Boston such as Samuel Adams, John Hancock, and Joseph Warren seem to have inspired the "tea party" of the night of December 16, 1773. An active participant among the lightly disguised "Mohawks" was Ebenezer Mackintosh, leader of Boston's South End Mob, who had spearheaded the Stamp Act riots of 1765. The Tea Party incited the British Parliament to pass the harsh Coercive Acts, which in turn caused Americans to react by convening the Continental Congress. The fateful chain of events came to a climax with the battles of Lexington and Concord, after which the Revolution was under way. Francis Rotch, mentioned in the narrative, was one of the tea-ship owners. Also mentioned in the account are John Rowe, a leading merchant and patriot; Dr. Thomas Young, another leading patriot; and Samuel Adams, the chief leader of the anti-British movement.

When Rotch returned and told the result of his application, it was nearly six o'clock. Darkness had set in, and the Old South, dimly lighted with candles, was still filled with an anxious and impatient multitude. "Who knows," said John Rowe, "how tea will mingle with salt water?" The people hurrahed vehemently, and the cry arose, "A mob! a mob!" A call to order restored quiet. Dr. Young then addressed the meeting, saying that Rotch was a good man, who had done all in his power to gratify the people, and charged them to do no hurt to his person or property.

From Francis S. Drake, Tea Leaves . . . *(Boston: A. O. Crane, 1884), pp. lxiii–lxv.*

To the final question then put to him, whether he would send his vessel back with the tea in her, under the present circumstances, he replied, that he could not, as he "apprehended that a compliance would prove his ruin." He also admitted that if called upon by the proper persons, he should attempt to land the tea for his own security.

Adams then arose and uttered the fateful words, "This meeting can do nothing more to save the country." This was doubtless the preconcerted signal for action, and it was answered by the men who sounded the war-whoop at the church door. The cry was re-echoed from the gallery, where a voice cried out, "Boston harbor a tea-pot to-night; hurrah for Griffin's wharf!" and the "Mohawks" passed on to cut the Gordian knot with their hatchets.

Silence was again commanded, when the people, after "manifesting a most exemplary patience and caution in the methods they had pursued to preserve the property of the East India Company, and to return it safe and untouched to its owners," perceiving that at every step they had been thwarted by the consignees and their coadjutors, then dissolved the meeting, giving three cheers as they dispersed.

Meanwhile a number of persons, variously estimated at from twenty to eighty (their number increasing as they advanced), some of them disguised as Indians, and armed with hatchets or axes, hurried to Griffin's (now Liverpool) wharf, boarded the ships, and, warning their crews and the customs officers to keep out of the way, in less than three hours time had broken and emptied into the dock three hundred and forty-two chests of tea, valued at £18,000. The deed was not that of a lawless mob, but the deliberate and well-considered act of intelligent, as well as determined, men. So careful were they not to destroy or injure private property, that they even replaced a padlock they had broken. There was no noise nor confusion. They worked so quietly and systematically that those on shore could distinctly hear the strokes of the hatchets. As soon as the people learned what was going forward, they made their way to the scene of operations, covering the wharves in the vicinity, whence they looked on in silence during the performance. The night was clear, the moon shone brilliantly, no one was harmed, and the town was never more quiet. Next day, the Dorchester shore was lined with tea, carried thither by the wind and tide. The serious spirit in which this deed was regarded by the leaders, is illustrated by the act of one who, after assisting his apprentice to disguise himself, dropped upon his knees and prayed fervently for his safety, and the success of the enterprise.

III

VIOLENCE IN
THE NINETEENTH CENTURY

7 / A Wave of Urban Riots, 1830–60

The 1830s, 1840s, and 1850s were a period of sustained urban rioting, particularly in the great cities of the northeast. It may have been the greatest era of urban violence that America has ever experienced. During this period at least 35 major riots and numerous minor ones occurred in four cities: Baltimore, Philadelphia, New York, and Boston. Baltimore had 12, Philadelphia had 11, New York had 8, and Boston had 4. Among the most important types of riots were labor riots (3), election riots (8), anti-abolitionist riots (4), anti-Negro riots (6), anti-Catholic riots (3), and riots of various sorts involving the unruly volunteer firemen units. The rise of the urban slum, exemplified by Five Points in lower Manhattan, with its restive lower-class residents had much to do with the frequent rioting. The lack of effective police forces in this era was another factor. Finally, the presence of a rapidly growing immigrant population—chiefly Irish Catholics—was at the bottom of much of the rioting. The Irish were often involved in violent confrontations with native American Protestants as a result of ethnic and religious hostility, and with Negroes as a result of competition for jobs and of racial prejudice. Examples of the wave of urban violence follow.

An Anti-Catholic Riot: The Burning of the Ursuline Convent in Charlestown, Massachusetts, August 11–12, 1834

The nation's first major anti-Catholic riot broke out in Charlestown, Massachusetts, on the night of August 11, 1834. Lower-class native American Protestants in Charlestown, a Boston suburb, resented the

33

presence of the convent school operated in their midst by the Ursuline sisters. The burning of the convent caused a sensation and triggered a generation of anti-Catholic violence and controversy that swept the country and was particularly acute in the large cities.

The turbulence fostered in the lower classes by the [Protestant] clergy found expression all through the early 1830's. In 1829 a group of Americans, aroused by the exhortations of a revivalistic preacher, attacked the homes of Irish Catholics in Boston and stoned them for three days. Four years later a group of drunken Irishmen beat a native American citizen to death on the streets of Charlestown. The next night five hundred natives marched on the Irish section, and troops that were called out stood helplessly by while a number of houses were torn down and burned. Posters warning of popish plots began to appear mysteriously about the streets of Charlestown and Boston. Rumors flew in increasing numbers concerning the convent on Mount Benedict: stories of barbarities practiced on the nuns, of a dying man cruelly treated, of the immorality with which it was infested. Parents who considered enrolling their daughters in the Ursuline school were subjected to pressure and plied with dreadful tales of convent life. An anti-Catholic novel, *The Nun,* which was popular just at this time, seemed to confirm many of these fears.

These rumors took on a new meaning with the actual appearance in Boston of an "escaped nun," Rebecca Theresa Reed, who had, according to her own tales, been a sister in the Ursuline convent. The fact that she had been known for years as a commonplace chit of a girl about Charlestown or that the Mother Superior of the Ursulines contended that she had merely been dismissed from a menial position in the sisterhood, did not dull the popular interest in her tales of convent life. Rebecca Reed's account of the dread occurrences within the walls of Mount Benedict and of the plots to carry her off to Canada to check her revelations were generally believed above all denials. Her tales prepared the people to believe the worst when an actual nun, Elizabeth Harrison, a member of the Ursuline order who taught music in the convent school, did "escape" a short time later. Overwork and long hours of teaching had undermined Miss Harrison's health to such an extent that she had become mentally deranged. In this condition, she left the convent on the night of July 28, 1834, ran to the home of a neighboring brick manufacturer, Edward Cutter, and demanded ref-

From *Ray Allen Billington,* The Protestant Crusade: 1800–1860 *(Chicago: Quadrangle Books, Inc., 1964), pp. 70–76. Copyright 1964 by Ray Allen Billington. Reprinted by permission of the author and the publisher.*

uge. Cutter took her to her brother in Cambridge, where reason returned, and Miss Harrison, realizing what she had done, immediately asked that Bishop Fenwick be sent for. He visited her the next day and readily granted her request to be allowed to return to the convent.

By that time, however, the mischief had been done. Before Miss Harrison was again at her accustomed post, all Boston had heard her story in an increasingly distorted form. It was generally believed that she had been forced to return and had been cast into a deep dungeon in the cellars of the convent building as punishment. These vague rumors probably would have been soon forgotten but for the publication of an article in one of the Boston papers, the *Mercantile Journal,* on the morning of August 8th, which stated:

MYSTERIOUS

We understand that a great excitement at present exists in Charlestown, in consequence of the mysterious disappearance of a young lady at the Nunnery in that place. The circumstances, as far as we can learn, are as follows: The young lady was sent to the place in question to complete her education, and became so pleased with the place and its inmates, that she was induced to seclude herself from the world and take the black veil. After some time spent in the Nunnery, she became dissatisfied, and made her escape from the institution—but was afterwards persuaded to return, being told that if she would continue but three weeks longer, she would be dismissed with honor. At the end of that time, a few days since, her friends called for her, but she was not to be found, and much alarm is excited in consequence.

These misstatements were copied in the *Morning Post* and the Boston *Commercial Gazette* and immediately caused a flurry of excitement among the sensation-loving populace. Placards were posted which called on the selectmen of Charlestown to investigate, threatening mob violence to the convent unless Miss Harrison was found. Feeling ran high both in Charlestown and Boston.

In the midst of this excitement, the Reverend Lyman Beecher returned to Boston, reaching the city during the week of August 3. On the night of Sunday, August 10, he delivered three violent anti-Catholic sermons in as many churches in Boston, exhorting overflowing audiences to action against Popery; an example which was followed by other Boston clergymen who were always ready to take advantage of the popular antipathy against Rome. Most of the city's pulpits on that Sabbath were given over to denunciations of Catholicism and many of the sermons were directed especially against the Ursuline convent.

In all probability the convent would have been attacked whether or not these sermons were delivered, for there is every reason to believe that the lower classes of Boston and Charlestown had agreed on its destruction even before Miss Harrison's escape and return. It seems clear that a group of truckmen and brickmakers had developed some sort of organization for this specific purpose, that they had held at least two meetings in which ways and means had been discussed, and that they had been prevented from acting before only by a lack of popular support. There is some indication that the leaders of this group were prominent Boston citizens, but this is by no means certain. It is fairly evident, however, that the existence of a plan to destroy the convent was well known among the lower classes at least three days before the actual burning took place and that no move was made against the rioters because public opinion in general gave tacit approval to the project.

Despite this conspiracy, proper action by the Charlestown selectmen would have done much to quell growing resentment and perhaps would have saved the convent. They were, however, unwilling to take any preventive steps because of a personal controversy with Bishop Fenwick in which they were then engaged. Bishop Fenwick had a short time before purchased three acres of land on Bunker Hill to be used as a Catholic cemetery and had applied to the selectmen for permission to bury two children there. The selectmen had replied that the health regulations of the town prevented the burial of any Roman Catholic, although allowing the burial of Protestants. Bishop Fenwick buried the children in the cemetery despite this refusal, and the selectmen brought suit against him. This litigation was pending when excitement over the convent reached its height, and made the selectmen little inclined to exert themselves in behalf of Catholics.

The growing feeling against the Mount Benedict institution finally convinced even the Charlestown selectmen that something must be done. On Saturday, August 9, they visited the convent building and asked to be allowed to make an inspection, but the Mother Superior, taking the attitude that they were responsible for many of the rumors, refused them admittance. However, Edward Cutter, who had sheltered Elizabeth Harrison during her mental derangement, was permitted to talk to Miss Harrison and satisfied himself that she was contented with her lot and not languishing in a hidden dungeon. On the following Monday, August 11, the selectmen were finally allowed to tour the building. They prepared a report for the Boston newspapers, stating that Miss Harrison was "entirely satisfied with her present situation, it being that of her own choice; and that she has no desire or wish to alter it." But when the papers published this report, together with one prepared by Cutter, on Tuesday morning, it was too late. The convent was then a mass of smoldering ruins.

A mob had begun to gather in the school grounds at nine o'clock on the night of August 11, carrying banners and shouting "No Popery" and "Down with the Cross." One Charlestown selectman was present and others were notified, but they insisted that the town's one police officer could handle the situation adequately. While the crowd was milling about, a group of forty or fifty men, evidently well organized and more or less disguised, approached the building and demanded that they be shown the nun who was secreted there. They were told to return the next day when the children would not be awakened and retired, seemingly satisfied. But at eleven o'clock a pile of tar barrels was lighted in a neighboring field, evidently a prearranged signal. Fire bells were set ringing and crowds of people began pouring into Charlestown. Fire companies appeared but stood helplessly by as the mob began the attack. The Mother Superior vainly tried to appeal to the throng, first by pleading, then by threatening that "the Bishop has twenty thousand Irishmen at his command in Boston." This only infuriated the crowd. Led by the same forty or fifty organized men who had been active from the first, they burst open the doors and entered the convent building as the dozen sisters present hurried the sixty pupils through a rear door and to a nearby place of refuge. At a little after midnight the torch was applied to both the school and a neighboring farmhouse belonging to the Ursulines. The large crowd stood by until both buildings were consumed by the flames.

Boston was thrown into a furor of excitement by the burning. Rumors spread that bands of Irishmen were marching on the city from neighboring railroad camps and Bishop Fenwick hurriedly dispatched six priests in as many directions to check this onslaught. The bishop also called Boston Catholics together and urged them to remain quiet and depend on the law to see that justice was done. These wise measures did not calm public fears, for everywhere people were apprehensive of some retaliatory step by the Irish and even the Harvard students appointed regular patrols to protect the Yard from attack or vandalism. "I have not," wrote a correspondent, "witnessed such a scene of excitement throughout the whole mass of the phlegmatic and peaceable population of Boston since my residence in the city commenced."

On the night after the attack a mob of men and boys marched to Mount Benedict, burned fences, trees, and all else they could find on the convent grounds, and were only kept from storming a nearby

Catholic church by the presence of troops stationed to guard the home of Edward Cutter. The next night a crowd of more than a thousand men wandered the streets of Boston, alarmed by a rumor that Irish laborers were descending on the city. On the following Friday, August 15, rioters burned a Charlestown shanty occupied by thirty-five Irish laborers, but further damage was averted when the drawbridge was raised to prevent the Boston mob which quickly formed from reaching the scene of the blaze.

An Ethnic War: Native Americans versus Irish Immigrants in the Philadephia Riot, May 3–8, 1844

By the middle of the 1840s the American nativist movement was well under way. Directed against immigrants, the movement actually invoked a combination of prejudices. The Irish Catholics, who were the main target of the nativists, were the victims of ethnic and anti-foreign prejudice because of their immigrant status; of religious prejudice because of their Catholic faith; of class prejudice because of their chiefly lower-class status; and of economic prejudice because lower-class native Protestants often competed with them for jobs. Philadelphia was a riot-torn city in the 1830s and 1840s; the nativist riot of May 3–8, 1844, was among the worst in that city. The inability of municipal authorities to cope with disorders like the Philadelphia riot of May 1844, was a direct cause leading to the formation of the modern urban police system in the years from 1844 to 1877. Volunteer firemen's companies were often a violent element in pre-Civil War urban life. The account below reveals the important role of such an organization, the Hibernia Hose Company.

During the early weeks of April a mounting tension was apparent among both Protestants and Catholics, particularly in the suburb of Kensington, an industrial section where Irish laborers were concentrated in large numbers. The first actual clash came late in the month, when a group of American Republicans announced that they would hold a meeting in the third ward of that city. Irish resentment at such an invasion of their territory was great, and threats were openly made that if the natives persisted in their intention, their meeting place would be burned to the ground. Undeterred by this warning, the na-

Billington, The Protestant Crusade, *pp. 222–26.*

tives assembled on the night of May 3, only to be routed by an Irish mob. Driven from their meeting, the remnants of the nativists gathered in a safe place and passed a series of resolutions:

> That we, the citizens of Kensington in mass meeting assembled, do solemnly protest against this flagrant violation of the rights of American citizens, and call upon our fellow citizens at large, to visit with their indignation and reproach, this outbreak of a vindictive, anti-republican spirit, manifested by a portion of the alien population of Third Ward Kensington.
>
> *Resolved,* That in view of the above transaction, we invite our fellow-citizens at large to attend the next meeting to sustain us in the expression of our opinions.
>
> *Resolved,* That when we adjourn we adjourn to meet in a mass meeting on Monday afternoon at 4 o'clock, at the corner of Second and Maseer [*sic*] streets.

This second meeting was little more than a gauntlet thrown at the feet of Irishmen ever eager to retrieve it. Bloodshed was being openly welcomed, nor was the situation eased by the attitude of the anti-Catholic press. On the morning of Monday, May 6, the day on which the postponed meeting was to be held, the *Native American* proclaimed:

NATIVE AMERICANS

> The American Republicans of the city and county of Philadelphia, who are determined to support the NATIVE AMERICANS in their Constitutional Rights of peaceably assembling to express their opinions on any question of Public Policy and to *Sustain them against the assaults of Aliens and Foreigners* are requested to assemble on THIS AFTERNOON, May 6th, 1844, at 4 o'clock, at the corner of Master and Second streets, Kensington, to express their indignation at the outrage on Friday evening last, and to take the necessary steps to prevent a repetition of it. *Natives be punctual and resolved to sustain your rights as Americans, firmly but moderately.*

Such an appeal would naturally attract rowdies from the lower classes, who would be ready to riot if given the slightest excuse.

Those who anticipated trouble were not disappointed. Several thousand strong, the American Republicans had scarcely gathered at the appointed meeting place when a heavy rain drove them in a bedraggled procession through the streets of the Irish section of Kensington to the Market House. Just as they were entering this building, several shots rang out, fired either from the windows of the Hibernia

Hose Company house, an Irish fire company, or from the mob itself. The meeting was thrown into a turmoil immediately. One of the marchers, a young man named George Shiffler, who had been struck and mortally wounded, was carried from the meeting by four men amid general confusion, where spectators were able to hear only one gray-haired man who shouted "On, On Americans. Liberty or Death." Before order could be restored, a band of Irish laborers stormed the building; the natives lost courage and made a hasty retreat for the second time.

Before nightfall another meeting of native Americans had been hurriedly assembled to lay plans for the burial of George Shiffler and the others who had been killed in the fighting. At its conclusion, those present again invaded the Irish quarter in Kensington and attacked several Irish homes before the militia arrived. "When the natives had got their blood up," one nativistic newspaper remarked with some bitterness, "and were fast gaining the ascendancy, the peace officers thought it high time to interpose the authority of the law."

The dawn of a new day found the whole city in the grip of intense excitement. Crowds gathered at every corner, listening to volunteer speakers exhort against Catholicism. A procession was hastily formed and marched through the streets bearing a torn American flag on which was painted: "This is the flag that was trampled under foot by the Irish papists." A proclamation by Bishop Kenrick deploring Catholic participation in the disorder did little good, for when copies were hurriedly posted throughout the city they were torn down and made into cockade hats by the natives. Two Irishmen, recognized as among the preceding night's rioters, were captured by a group of Americans and taken to an alderman's home while a mob followed at their heels shouting, "Kill them. Kill them. Blood for blood." The editor of the *Native American* completely lost his sense of balance; his paper, appearing with its columns shrouded in black, boldly demanded reprisal and more bloodshed:

Heretofore we have been among those who have entered our solemn protest against any observations that would bear the slightest semblance of making the Native cause a religious one, or charging upon our adopted fellow-citizens any other feeling than that of a mistaken opinion as to our views and their own rights. We hold back no longer. We are now free to declare that *no terms whatever* are to be held with these people.

Another St. Bartholomew's days is begun on the streets of Philadelphia. The bloody hand of the Pope has stretched itself forth to our destruction. We now call on our fellow-citizens, who regard free institutions, whether they be native or adopted, to arm. Our liberties are now to be fought for;—let us not be slack in our preparations.

Spurred on by this ill-advised warning, native Americans assembled that afternoon in the State House yard. Orators tried to warn them against bloodshed and cautioned them to keep the peace, but their words were answered by cries of "No, No," from the crowd. After adopting a number of resolutions asserting the right of peaceful assembly and charging the Papists with an attempt to drive the Bible from the schools, the natives banded together and again marched into Kensington. Traversing the Irish section shouting insults and damaging Irish homes, the mob was soon locked in armed conflict with equally riotous foreigners. The Hibernia Hose Company house was stormed and demolished; before midnight more than thirty houses belonging to Irishmen had been burned to the ground, and only the tardy arrival of the militia put an end to the holocaust.

The third day of rioting climaxed this period of disorder. Crowds began gathering on the streets of Kensington early in the afternoon, shouting against the Pope and demanding vengeance for the natives who had been killed. To observers many of the attackers seemed to be well organized and bent solely on the systematic destruction of Irish homes, for within a few hours whole blocks of houses were in flames. The militia appeared but proved powerless before the pillaging mob. Protestant Irish and Americans all over Kensington hastened to protect themselves by fastening large signs bearing the legend "Native American" upon the doors of their houses, or lacking these, hastily displaying a copy of the newspaper of that name. The crowd always stopped before such a sign to cheer.

Roaming the streets, the rioters finally came to Saint Michael's Catholic church. A rumor that arms were concealed within the building proved sufficient grounds for attack, and while the presiding priest fled in disguise, the torch was applied. As flames consumed the church and an adjoining seminary, the rioters marched on St. Augustine's church. A hurry call was dispatched for the mayor, who had been neglecting his duties to celebrate his daughter's birthday, but his speech to the crowd from the steps of the structure, in which he stated that the building was unarmed and that he himself had the key, had an opposite effect from that intended. The mob, now assured that the building was not defended, brushed past the few militia available, burst open the doors, and set fire to the church. Throughout the city priests and nuns trembled for their lives, and Kensington was fast assuming the aspect of a war-torn town as Irish refugees fled with their belongings.

The burning of Saint Augustine's church marked the peak of mob rule. Philadelphia awakened on the morning of May 9, sobered by a chorus of criticism resounding throughout the nation. "Who would not give worlds," wrote the editor of the *Spirit of the Times,* "to wipe off the foul blot from the disgraced name of our city? . . ." Even the *Native American* appeared in chastened form, declaring: "No terms that we can use are able to express the deep reprobation that we feel for this iniquitous proceeding; this wanton and uncalled for desecration of the Christian altar." A mass meeting, called at the insistence of the mayor, met that afternoon and agreed to the appointment of special policemen in each ward to keep order. These officers were immediately sworn in and patrolled the streets of Kensington all that night. There was no further evidence of trouble and quiet seemed to have settled on a mollified and sobered Philadelphia.

An Election Riot in "Mob Town" (Baltimore), 1856

Down to the 1860s Baltimore was one of the most violent of all American cities. A tremendous anti-Federalist riot in 1812 earned it the nickname of "Mob Town," a label that it more than lived up to in the period from 1834 to 1862, during which it was wracked by 15 major riots. The riots stemmed from diverse causes: political, economic, ethnic, labor, and Civil War tensions. In the pre-Civil War period (and as late as the 1930s) election day in American localities was often an occasion of sharp violence. Baltimore was no exception. It had major election riots in 1848, 1856 (two), 1858, and 1859. The following description of the Baltimore riot of November 4, 1856, not only typifies election-day violence in "Mob Town" but also illustrates the sharp fighting that often broke out in the 1850s between urban Democrats, who were often Irish Catholics, and the native American Protestant members of the Know-Nothing Party. In this riot eight were killed and some 150 were wounded as virtual guerrilla warfare scorched the streets of the Chesapeake metropolis.

Our city, on the 4th of November, was again made the theatre of the most prolonged and desperate rioting. Armed and organized associations, belonging to both political parties, resorted to firearms, with which they were liberally provided, and fought with ferocious and daring recklessness. Individual combats and minor affrays occurred at

From John Thomas Scharf, The Chronicles of Baltimore . . . (*Baltimore: Turnbull Bros., 1874), pp. 550–52.*

a number of polls, but the most serious took place in the vicinity of the second and eighth ward polls. In both of these riots eight persons were killed and about 150 were wounded.

During the morning there was considerable ill-feeling displayed at the second ward polls, but up to three o'clock no serious disturbance occurred. At that hour a furious fight broke out, said to have originated from a stone being thrown into the crowd surrounding the window. Pistols were immediately drawn and fired by both parties. The Democrats drove the Know-Nothings from the polls and up High street. The alarm was carried to the fourth ward polls, and a strong body of Know-Nothings started from there. In the vicinity of the second ward polls they were met and driven back. Further reinforcements were then received and the battle renewed. A good proportion of both parties by this time were provided with muskets, whilst others used pistols, and others skirmished with knives and clubs. Both parties fought with determination, and in many instances exposed themselves with the most reckless disregard of danger. The battle-ground was spread over portions of Fawn, Stiles, Exeter and High streets, and Eastern Avenue, and the spectacle presented was a terrible and revolting one. As either party gained a temporary advantage, men would be seen running, with others shooting at them; the wounded were limping off and being carried away by their companions, whilst others begrimed with smoke and powder, and in some cases covered with blood, still kept up the fight, now firing singly and then again in volleys. In the surrounding neighborhood the utmost degree of excitement and consternation prevailed. Children were hastily gathered, the houses closed, and the occupants in many instances sought their garrets and cellars to be out of harm's way. The Democrats were finally overpowered, driven away from the polls, and retreated, still fighting, down Eastern Avenue. In the neighborhood of the Causeway they again made a stand, and there a guerilla warfare, carried on from the alleys and street corners, continued for more than an hour. About 3 o'clock in the afternoon a report was brought to the police stationed at the eighth ward, that there was fighting at the sixth ward, and assistance was asked to quell it. The police started, and with them several hundred of the crowd assembled around the polls, who in a few moments were armed with muskets, and accompanied by two gangs of boys, each dragging small brass cannon on wheels. They passed along the side of the Belair market, and towards Orleans street, when they were met by a concourse of equally as wild infuriated men and youths, armed with muskets and pistols. A fight then commenced, the eighth ward Democrats taking shelter in the market-house, and the sixth and seventh ward Know-Nothings firing from the fish-market and the corner of Orleans street. They finally rallied on the eighth ward party and drove them up through the market, accompanied by perfect volleys of musketry and the occasional discharge of a swivel. The fighting through the market was continued with but little intermission up to dark, when both parties retired. The scene in the vicinity of the Belair market was of the most sanguinary character throughout the afternoon. At times one party would apparently obtain the better of the other, and they continued to drive each other back and forward through the market-house. The sixth ward party were reinforced shortly after the battle commenced by a detachment of the seventh ward and other Know-Nothing clubs, who brought with them a small cannon on wheels. The Democrats got possession of this cannon at one time, and were about carrying it off, when it upset and the cannon fell off the wheels. Whilst the fight was going on in the Belair market, word was sent to the central station for aid. High constable Herring, deputy Brashears, and Sergeant Tayman, with a squad of twenty men, repaired to the scene. On arriving at the market they found the eighth warders with a cannon in position preparing to fire. They attempted to take possession of the piece, but were immediately surrounded by an infuriated crowd armed with muskets. They attempted to make arrests, but were foiled by the number and fierceness of the assailants, but succeeded, however, in carrying off the cannon.

8 / A Slave Rebellion from a Black Perspective: Nat Turner's Confession, 1831

America's greatest slave rebellion took place in the Tidewater region of southeastern Virginia in Southampton County. On August 22–23, 1831, Nat Turner led 60–80 Negroes in an uprising that took 55–65 white lives. The insurrection was suppressed with great severity by white military units and volunteers. Many apparently innocent Negroes were killed. Later, Turner and 19 other Negroes were executed. Turner was hanged on November 11, 1831. Turner's confession to the white man, Thomas R. Gray, follows.

Sir,—You have asked me to give a history of the motives which induced me to undertake the late insurrection, as you call it—To do so

From Thomas R. Gray, The Confessions of Nat Turner . . . (*Baltimore: Thomas R. Gray, 1831*), pp. 7, 9, 11–18.

I must go back to the days of my infancy, and even before I was born. I was thirty-one years of age the 2nd of October last, and born the property of Benj. Turner, of this county. In my childhood a circumstance occurred which made an indelible impression on my mind, and laid the ground work of that enthusiasm, which has terminated so fatally to many, both white and black, and for which I am about to atone at the gallows. It is here necessary to relate this circumstance—trifling as it may seem, it was the commencement of that belief which has grown with time, and even now, sir, in this dungeon, helpless and forsaken as I am, I cannot divest myself of. Being at play with other children, when three or four years old, I was telling them something, which my mother overhearing, said it had happened before I was born—I stuck to my story, however, and related somethings which went, in her opinion, to confirm it—others being called on were greatly astonished, knowing that these things had happened, and caused them to say in my hearing, I surely would be a prophet, as the Lord had shewn me things that had happened before my birth. And my father and mother strengthened me in this my first impression, saying in my presence, I was intended for some great purpose. . . . [H]aving arrived to man's estate, and hearing the scriptures commented on at meetings, I was struck with that particular passage which says: "Seek ye the kingdom of Heaven and all things shall be added unto you." I reflected much on this passage, and prayed daily for light on this subject—As I was praying one day at my plough, the spirit spoke to me, saying "Seek ye the kingdom of Heaven and all things shall be added unto you." . . .

And on the 12th of May, 1828, I heard a loud noise in the heavens, and the Spirit instantly appeared to me and said the Serpent was loosened, and Christ had laid down the yoke he had borne for the sins of men, and that I should take it on and fight against the Serpent, for the time was fast approaching when the first should be last and the last should be first. . . . And by signs in the heavens that it would make known to me when I should commence the great work—and until the first sign appeared, I should conceal it from the knowledge of men—And on the appearance of the sign, (the eclipse of the sun last February) I should arise and prepare myself, and slay my enemies with their own weapons. And immediately on the sign appearing in the heavens, the seal was removed from my lips, and I communicated the great work laid out for me to do, to four in whom I had the greatest confidence, (Henry, Hark, Nelson, and Sam)—It was intended by us to have begun the work of death on the 4th July last—Many were the plans formed and rejected by us, and it affected my mind to such a degree, that I fell sick, and the time passed without our coming to any determination how to commence—Still forming new schemes and rejecting them, when the sign appeared again, which determined me not to wait longer.

Since the commencement of 1830, I had been living with Mr. Joseph Travis, who was to me a kind master, and placed the greatest confidence in me; in fact, I had no cause to complain of his treatment to me. On Saturday evening, the 20th of August, it was agreed between Henry, Hark and myself, to prepare a dinner the next day for the men we expected, and then to concert a plan, as we had not yet determined on any. Hark, on the following morning, brought a pig, and Henry brandy, and being joined by Sam, Nelson, Will and Jack, they prepared in the woods a dinner, where, about three o'clock, I joined them. . . .

I saluted them on coming up, and asked Will how came he there, he answered, his life was worth no more than others, and his liberty as dear to him. I asked him if he thought to obtain it? He said he would, or lose his life. This was enough to put him in full confidence. Jack, I knew, was only a tool in the hands of Hark, it was quickly agreed we should commence at home (Mr. J. Travis') on that night, and until we had armed and equipped ourselves, and gathered sufficient force, neither age nor sex was to be spared, (which was invariably adhered to).

We remained at the feast, until about two hours in the night, when we went to the house and found Austin; they all went to the cider press and drank, except myself. On returning to the house, Hark went to the door with an axe, for the purpose of breaking it open, as we knew we were strong enough to murder the family, if they were awaked by the noise; but reflecting that it might create an alarm in the neighborhood, we determined to enter the house secretly, and murder them whilst sleeping. Hark got a ladder and set it against the chimney, on which I ascended, and hoisting a window, entered and came down stairs, unbarred the door, and removed the guns from their places.

It was then observed that I must spill the first blood. On which, armed with a hatchet, and accompanied by Will, I entered my master's chamber, it being dark, I could not give a death blow, the hatchet glanced from his head, he sprang from the bed and called his wife, it was his last word, Will laid him dead, with a blow of his axe, and Mrs. Travis shared the same fate, as she lay in bed. The murder of this family, five in number, was the work of a moment, not one of them awoke; there was a little infant sleeping in a cradle, that was forgotten, until we had left the house and gone some distance, when Henry and Will returned and killed it; we got here, four guns that would shoot, and several old muskets, with a pound or two of powder.

We remained some time at the barn, where we paraded; I formed them in a line as soldiers, and after carrying them through all the manoeuvres I was master of marched them off to Mr. Salathul Francis,' about six hundred yards distant. Sam and Will went to the door and knocked. Mr. Francis asked who was there, Sam replied it was him, and he had a letter for him, on which he got up and came to the door; they immediately seized him, and dragging him out a little from the door, he was dispatched by repeated blows on the head; there was no other white person in the family. We started from there for Mrs. Reese's, maintaining the most perfect silence on our march, where finding the door unlocked, we entered, and murdered Mrs. Reese in her bed, while sleeping; her son awoke, but it was only to sleep the sleep of death, he had only time to say who is that, and he was no more.

From Mrs. Reese's we went to Mrs. Turner's, a mile distant, which we reached about sunrise, on Monday morning. Henry, Austin, and Sam, went to the still, where, finding Mr. Peebles, Austin shot him, and the rest of us went to the house; as we approached, the family discovered us, and shut the door. Vain hope! Will, with one stroke of his axe, opened it, and we entered and found Mrs. Turner and Mrs. Newsome in the middle of a room, almost frightened to death. Will immediately killed Mrs. Turner, with one blow of his axe. I took Mrs. Newsome by the hand, and with the sword I had when I was apprehended, I struck her several blows over the head, but not being able to kill her, as the sword was dull. Will turning around and discovered it, despatched her also. A general destruction of property and search for money and ammunition, always succeeded the murders.

By this time my company amounted to fifteen, and nine men mounted, who started for Mrs. Whitehead's (the other six were to go through a by way to Mr. Bryant's, and rejoin us at Mrs. Whitehead's); as we approached the house we discovered Mr. Richard Whitehead standing in the cotton patch, near the lane fence; we called him over into the lane, and Will, the executioner, was near at hand, with his fatal axe, to send him to an untimely grave. As we pushed on to the house, I discovered some one run round the garden, and thinking it was some of the white family, I pursued them, but finding it was a servant girl belonging to the house, I returned to commence the work of death, but they whom I left, had not been idle; all the family were already murdered, but Mrs. Whitehead and her daughter Margaret.

As I came round to the door I saw Will pulling Mrs. Whitehead out of the house, and at the step he nearly severed her head from her body, with his broad axe. Miss Margaret, when I discovered her, had concealed herself in the corner, formed by the projection of cellar cap from the house; on my approach she fled, but was soon overtaken, and after repeated blows with a sword, I killed her by a blow on the head, with a fence rail. By this time, the six who had gone by Mr. Bryant's, rejoined us, and informed me they had done the work of death assigned them.

We again divided, part going to Mr. Richard Porter's, and from thence to Nathaniel Francis,' the others to Mr. Howell Harris,' and Mr. T. Doyles. On my reaching Mr. Porter's, he had escaped with his family. I understood there, that the alarm had already spread, and I immediately returned to bring up those sent to Mr. Doyles,' and Mr. Howell Harris'; the party I left going on to Mr. Francis,' having told them I would join them in that neighborhood. I met these sent to Mr. Doyles' and Mr. Harris' returning, having met Mr. Doyle on the road and killed him; and learning from some who joined them, that Mr. Harris was from home, I immediately pursued the course taken by the party gone on before; but knowing they would complete the work of death and pillage, at Mr. Francis' before I could get there, I went to Mr. Peter Edwards,' expecting to find them there, but they had been here also. I then went to Mr. John T. Barrow's, they had been here and murdered him. I pursued on their track to Capt. Newit Harris,' where I found the greater part mounted, and ready to start; the men now amounting to about forty, shouted and hurraed as I rode up, some were in the yard, loading their guns, others drinking. They said Captain Harris and his family had escaped, the property in the house they destroyed, robbing him of money and other valuables. I ordered them to mount and march instantly, this was about nine or ten o'clock, Monday morning.

I proceeded to Mr. Levi Waller's, two or three miles distant. I took my station in the rear, and as it was my object to carry terror and devastation wherever we went, I placed fifteen or twenty of the best armed and most relied on, in front, who generally approached the houses as fast as their horses could run; this was for two purposes, to prevent escape and strike terror to the inhabitants—on this account I never got to the houses, after leaving Mrs. Whitehead's, until the murders were committed, except in one case. I sometimes got in sight in time to see the work of death completed, viewed the mangled bodies as they lay, in silent satisfaction, and immediately started in quest of other victims—Having murdered Mrs. Waller and ten children, we started for Mr. William Williams'—having killed him and two little boys that were there; while engaged in this, Mrs. Williams fled and got some distance from the house, but she was pursued, overtaken, and compelled to get up behind one of the company, who brought her back, and after showing her the mangled body of her lifeless husband, she was told to get down and lay by his side, where she was shot dead.

I then started for Mr. Jacob Williams, where the family were murdered—Here he found a young man named Drury, who had come on business with Mr. Williams—he was pursued, overtaken and shot. Mrs. Vaughan was the next place we visited—and after murdering the family here, I determined on starting for Jerusalem[1]—Our number amounted now to fifty or sixty, all mounted and armed with guns, axes, swords and clubs—On reaching Mr. James W. Parker's gate, immediately on the road leading to Jerusalem, and about three miles distant, it was proposed to me to call there, but I objected, as I knew he was gone to Jerusalem, and my object was to reach there as soon as possible; but some of the men having relations at Mr. Parker's it was agreed that they might call and get his people. I remained at the gate on the road, with seven or eight; the others going across the field to the house, about half a mile off.

After waiting some time for them, I became impatient, and started to the house for them, and on our return we were met by a party of white men, who had pursued our blood-stained track, and who had fired on those at the gate, and dispersed them, which I knew nothing of, not having been at that time rejoined by any of them—Immediately on discovering the whites, I ordered my men to halt and form, as they appeared to be alarmed—The white men, eighteen in number, approached us in about one hundred yards, when one of them fired. . . .—And I discovered about half of them retreating, I then ordered my men to fire and rush on them; the few remaining stood their ground until we approached within fifty yards, when they fired and retreated.

We pursued and overtook some of them who we thought we left dead; . . . after pursuing them about two hundred yards, and rising a little hill, I discovered they were met by another party, and had halted, and were re-loading their guns. . . . Thinking that those who retreated first, and the party who fired on us at fifty or sixty yards distant, had all fallen back to meet others with ammunition. As I saw them reloading their guns, and more coming up than I saw at first, and several of my bravest men being wounded, the others became panick

---

[1] [Jerusalem was the county seat. In 1888 its name was changed to Courtland.]

struck and squandered over the field; the white men pursued and fired on us several times. Hark had his horse shot under him, and I caught another for him as it was running by me; five or six of my men were wounded, but none left on the field; finding myself defeated here I instantly determined to go through a private way, and cross the Nottoway river at the Cypress Bridge, three miles below Jerusalem, and attack that place in the rear, as I expected they would look for me on the other road, and I had a great desire to get there to procure arms and ammunition.

After going a short distance in this private way, accompanied by about twenty men, I overtook two or three who told me the others were dispersed in every direction. After trying in vain to collect a sufficient force to proceed to Jerusalem, I determined to return, as I was sure they would make back to their old neighborhood, where they would rejoin me, make new recruits, and come down again. On my way back, I called at Mrs. Thomas's, Mrs. Spencer's, and several other places, the white families having fled, we found no more victims to gratify our thirst for blood, we stopped at Majr. Ridley's quarter for the night, and being joined by four of his men, with the recruits made since my defeat, we mustered now about forty strong.

After placing our sentinels, I laid down to sleep, but was quickly roused by a great racket; starting up, I found some mounted, and others in great confusion; one of the sentinels having given the alarm that we were about to be attacked, I ordered some to ride round and reconnoitre, and on their return the others being more alarmed, not knowing who they were, fled in different ways, so that I was reduced to about twenty again; with this I determined to attempt to recruit, and proceed on to rally in the neighborhood, I had left.

Dr. Blunt's was the nearest house, which we reached just before day; on riding up the yard, Hark fired a gun. We expected Dr. Blunt and his family were at Maj. Ridley's, as I knew there was a company of men there; the gun was fired to ascertain if any of the family were at home; we were immediately fired upon and retreated, leaving several of my men. I do not know what became of them, as I never saw them afterwards. Pursuing our course back and coming in sight of Captain Harris,' where we had been the day before, we discovered a party of white men at the house, on which all deserted me but two, (Jacob and Nat), we concealed ourselves in the woods until near night, when I sent them in search of Henry, Sam, Nelson, and Hark, and directed them to rally all they could, at the place we had had our dinner the Sunday before, where they would find me, and I accordingly returned there as soon as it was dark and remained until Wednesday evening, when discovering white men riding around the place as though they were looking for some one, and none of my men joining me, I concluded Jacob and Nat had been taken, and compelled to betray me.

On this I gave up all hope for the present; and on Thursday night after having supplied myself with provisions from Mr. Travis's, I scratched a hole under a pile of fence rails in a field, where I concealed myself for six weeks, never leaving my hiding place but for a few minutes in the dead of night to get water which was very near; thinking by this time I could venture out, I began to go about in the night and eaves drop the houses in the neighborhood; pursuing this course for about a fortnight and gathering little or no intelligence, afraid of speaking to any human being, and returning every morning to my cave before the dawn of day.

I know not how long I might have led this life, if accident had not betrayed me, a dog in the neighborhood passing by my hiding place one night while I was out, was attracted by some meat I had in my cave, and crawled in and stole it, and was coming out just as I returned. A few nights after, two negroes having started to go hunting with the same dog, and passed that way, the dog came again to the place, and having just gone out to walk about, discovered me and barked, on which thinking myself discovered, I spoke to them to beg concealment. On making myself known they fled from me. Knowing then they would betray me, I immediately left my hiding place, and was pursued almost incessantly until I was taken a fortnight afterwards by Mr. Benjamin Phipps, in a little hole I had dug out with my sword, for the purpose of concealment, under the top of a fallen tree. On Mr. Phipps' discovering the place of my concealment, he cocked his gun and aimed at me. I requested him not to shoot and I would give up, upon which he demanded my sword. I delivered it to him, and he brought me to prison. I am here loaded with chains, and willing to suffer the fate that awaits me.

Thomas R. Gray, to whom Nat Turner gave his account of the rebellion, wrote the following about Nat.

It has been said he was ignorant and cowardly, and that his object was to murder and rob for the purpose of obtaining money to make his escape. It is notorious, that he was never known to have a dollar in his life; to swear an oath, or drink a drop of spirits. As to his ignorance, he certainly never had the advantages of education, but he can read

Gray, Confessions, *pp. 18–19.*

and write, (it was taught him by his parents,) and for natural intelligence and quickness of apprehension, is surpassed by few men I have ever seen. As to his being a coward, his reason as given for not resisting Mr. Phipps, shews the decision of his character. When he saw Mr. Phipps present his gun, he said he knew it was impossible for him to escape as the woods were full of men; he therefore thought it was better to surrender, and trust to fortune for his escape. He is a complete fanatic, or plays his part most admirably. On other subjects he possesses an uncommon share of intelligence, with a mind capable of attaining any thing; but warped and perverted by the influence of early impressions. He is below the ordinary stature, though strong and active, having the true negro face, every feature of which is strongly marked.

9 / Agrarian Violence: The New York Anti-Rent Disturbances, 1844–45

The anti-rent movement of upstate New York was a revolt by small farmers against the tenant system, which the farmers felt to be excessively burdensome, especially in an era of agricultural decline in the uplands of the Hudson-Mohawk region. The disturbances began in the late colonial period, flared again in 1839, reached a peak in the middle 1840s, and continued sporadically for some time after the Civil War. Of the many American movements of agrarian violence, the anti-rent movement—which spanned two centuries—has been unequaled for sustained violence. Hearkening back to the patriotic "Mohawks" who dumped British tea in Boston harbor as a prelude to the American Revolution, the Anti-Rent insurgents disguised themselves as Indians. In 1844–45 full-scale uprisings occurred in Albany, Columbia, Schoharie, and Delaware counties. The selection that follows illustrates the violent fervor of the anti-renters. It relates the killing of Deputy Sheriff Osman N. Steele by anti-renters in Delaware County on August 7, 1845. Steele was killed for attempting to sell the farm of tenant Moses Earle, who was two years in arrears on his rent. The sale was to reimburse the landlord for defaulted rent and the expense of collecting it. The sensational shooting of Steele resulted in the occupation of the area by state militia and a mass trial of anti-renters. The violence subsided as the anti-rent movement emphasized reform through political means.

From the Albany Argus, *August 11, 1845, p. 2.*

We have at length the climax of outrage and murder in this county. The "Indians," as they are called—disguised whites, who appropriately assume the name of 'Indians'—yesterday not only resisted the lawful authorities, but wantonly shot down deputy sheriff Steele, a valuable and highly esteemed citizen and officer; and here all is excitement and the highest feeling. The circumstances of this transaction, which blackens the character of our hitherto peaceful and order-loving county, are as follows: . . .

Some weeks ago a warrant was issued to Green Moore, Sheriff of Delaware county, by John Allen, the agent of Charlotte D. Verplanck, the owner of a few lots in great lot No. 39, in the Hardenburgh patent, to collect $64, being two years' rent in arrear, on a farm of 160 acres. The sale of the property levied on, which was to have taken place on the 7th. . . .

P. P. Wright testified that he left Delhi in company with sheriff Moore on the morning of the 6th inst., for Shavertown, intending to go with him the next day to Moses Earle's in Andes, to attend the sale of the property which had been distrained for rent due to Charlotte D. Verplanck.

. . . The sheriff and witness [Wright] arrived at Earle's about 10 o'clock; there were some spectators and some men mowing [*sic*] on the lower side of the road; the sheriff and witness then went to see Earle and asked him if the rent could not be settled; Earle said no, he would not settle it, but would fight it out the hardest.

. . . afterwards witness saw about 50 Indians come out of the woods in Indian file, disguised and armed; soon afterwards saw a body of men come from the north side of the road and pass to the south; these halted, when they got 3 or 4 rods into the lot. The Chief motioned towards witness, and said "tory, tory"; there were 14 of these, some of whom had their masks turned up. About half-past 12, (the sale was to take place at 1 o'clock,) they commenced marching out of the woods through a pasture, and through the bars into the road; witness thought there were about 100; they went down the road, and formed a single line in the road; about 8 or 9 rods long. . . .

The Indians were then provided with refreshments from Earle's house; they asked witness if he intended to bid; witness told them he should, if the property was offered; one Indian then said, "If you do, you will go home in a wagon, feet foremost," and a bystander responded, "that's the talk." Soon after, officers Osman N. Steele and Erastus S. Edgerton came up, it being then about two o'clock; witness and they promised to stand by each other. The sheriff announced that he would proceed to sell, and went after the property, accompanied by Mr. Burr and others; twelve Indians went down with them; they were in full disguise and all armed, most having rifles, some swords, pistols, tomahawks, &c.

The sheriff drove the cattle up by the bars; the Indians then came into the lot and formed a hollow square around the property and guarded the bars with a platoon of Indians, to prevent citizens and bidders from coming into the lot; witness called to the sheriff saying that the bidders were all in the road and the property must come there, where the bidders were, or he would be required to postpone the sale; the sheriff then talked with the Indians about it, and was attempting to get the property into the road; Wm. Brisbane told witness he tho't the sheriff had no right to take the property into the road; witness then consulted with Steele and Edgerton as to the course to be pursued, and witness asked them to go down to the barn and look at the advertisement, and see where the property was to be sold; they started to go there; at this time about 15 Indians ran out of the lot and were crossing the road into another field, as if they were attempting to head Steele and Edgerton, thinking they were about starting for home; they returned, and the Indians then moved back into the lot, passing through the bars again, and formed in the square, a file of Indians still being at the bars, which were down; Steele and Edgerton were behind witness on horseback, witness being on foot; witness attempted to pass the bars, and the Indians forbid his entrance; he told them it was a public sale and he should pass in; by shoving against an Indian he effected an entrance into the lot; officers Steele and Edgerton immediately followed, and passed into the lot about one or two lengths of their horses; the Chief then gave the command, *"Shoot the horses"*, this was repeated by several; Edgerton then proclaimed in a loud voice, *"I command every citizen to assist in the preservation of the peace,"* at the same time the Indians cried out, *"Shoot the horses—shoot him, shoot him!"* The Indians at the same time forming around witness and Steele and Edgerton a semicircle of 15 or 20 feet radius, enclosing them there, and discharging a volley of rifles at them.

Witness instantly perceived the effect in the breast of Edgerton's horse; saw Steele with his pistol drawn, his arm appearing to be disabled; in less than one-fourth of a minute another volley was discharged upon them, proving fatal to Steele, and both horses. Edgerton's horse was shot through the saddle, and fell, Edgerton jumping off. Steele fell instantly from his horse, which fell over in another direction; three balls passed through Steele's body. The Sheriff and Edgerton and witness ran up to Steele, and he said: "I am a dead man—I am shot two or three times through the bowels." . . .

Steele was laid on a bed, in intense agony. He spoke to Earle, and said: "If you had settled your rent, I should not have been shot, but now I have lost my life." Earle replied, *"he should not settle the rent, if it cost forty lives."* Witness remained with Steele; he was shot at half past two, and died a little after eight o'clock. When Steele first came up in the road, the Indians commenced blackguarding him, and continued it while he was in the road; Steele made no reply or remark to them, but was peaceable.

10 / Whites Slaughtered by Indians: The Sioux Uprising in Minnesota, 1862

Among the most ferocious and successful of Indian uprisings was that of the Sioux in Minnesota in 1862. Various grievances having to do with land transactions and food supplies, among others, caused the Indians to begin the massacre on August 18, 1862. Mixed forces of federal troops and state militia defeated the Indians in the fall of 1862, but before then from 450 to 750 whites had been killed, property damage of from $1 million to $2.5 million had been inflicted, and 30,000 settlers had been forced to flee the Minnesota River valley. The following narrative of Mary Schwandt describes the suffering of the settlers—a burden that bore especially hard upon pioneer women and children, just as it had ever since the seventeenth century. A by-product of the uprising was the mass hanging of 38 Indians on one gallows. It was probably the largest mass hanging in America.

Narrative of Mary Schwandt

On the morning of the 18th of August, Mattie Williams, Mary Anderson, Mr. Patoile, Mr. L. Davis, a Frenchman, and myself, put our clothing into a two-horse wagon and started for New Ulm. When we arrived at John Moore's, a half-breed, we were informed that the Indians were killing all the whites on Beaver Creek and Sacred Heart, and were advised to keep off from the road and follow Mr. Reynolds, who had gone on ahead of us. . . .

From *Charles S. Bryant,* A History of the Great Massacre by the Sioux Indians . . . (*Cincinnati: Rickey & Carroll, 1864*), *pp. 336, 338–41.*

When we arrived opposite the fort, Mr. Patoile, supposing we could not cross the river, as there was no ferry there, continued down on the New Ulm road. The horses were now very tired, and we frequently got out and walked. When within about eight miles of New Ulm, some fifty Indians, with horses and wagons, and barrels full of flour, and all sorts of goods and pictures, taken from the houses, came from the direction of that town. They seemed to be all drunk, were very noisy, and perfectly naked, and painted all over their bodies. Two of them, on horseback, came on ahead of the rest, one on each side of us, and ordered us to stop. The team was turned out of the road, and all but Patoile jumped out of the wagon. They came up and shot him, some four balls entering his body, and he fell out of the wagon dead, and they left him lying there.

The rest of us ran toward the woods and hid in a slough, in the tall grass. The men were both killed in the slough. When we jumped from the wagon, Davis exclaimed, "We are lost!" I heard nothing said by any one else. The Frenchman ran in a different direction from where we were. I have a faint recollection of seeing him fall when he was shot. Mr. Davis was with us, and was shot about the same time. Mary Anderson was away behind us, and was shot through the lower part of the body, the ball entering at the hip and coming out through the abdomen. She was not killed, and the Indians must have carried her to the wagon, as, when I again saw her, she was in a wagon, being drawn by one of the savages. As they came toward us we screamed, when one of them took hold of Mattie and tore off her "shaker," and two took hold of me, one hold of each arm, and forced us back to the wagon. They put Mattie in the wagon with Mary, and me in another, driven by the negro Godfrey. The wagon with Mattie and Mary went toward the Agency, and the one I was in went off into the prairie.

I asked Godfrey what they were going to do with me. He said he did not know. He told me they had chased Mr. and Mrs. Reynolds, and, he thought, had killed them. About two or three miles out on the prairie, we came to the squaws, for whom Godfrey told me they were looking. Here we all sat down, and the squaws took bread from the wagons, and all ate; and the Indians fixed up their hair, and tied it up with ribbons.

It was now about five o'clock. We remained where we were about one hour, and then went on to the house of Waucouta, a chief of the Wapekuta tribe, about half a mile from the Agency. Here I found Mrs. J. W. De Camp, who, with her two children, was captured at the Lower Agency. It was about eight o'clock when we arrived at Waucouta's house, and the buildings were still burning at the Agency when

we got there. We could see them plainly from where we were. I had
been there about half an hour when an Indian came, whom Mrs.
De Camp supposed to be friendly, as he was a farmer Indian, and,
fearing others would come and abuse us, she asked him to stay. After
awhile a number more came, and, after annoying me with their loathsome attentions for a long time, one of them laid his hands forcibly
upon me, when I screamed, and one of the fiends struck me on my
mouth with his hand, causing the blood to flow very freely. They then
took me out by force, to an unoccupied tepee, near the house, and
perpetrated the most horrible and nameless outrages upon my person. These outrages were repeated, at different times during my
captivity. . . .

At ten or eleven o'clock, Mattie and Mary Anderson came. The ball
was yet in Mary's body, and Waucouta tried to cut it out, but failed.
Mary then took the knife from the hand of Waucouta, and removed it
herself. We remained here some four days. Cold water was poured
upon corn-meal for Mary to drink, but we had nothing to eat, except
some potatoes we dug in the garden, for those four days. On the fourth
day we went to the camp of Little Crow. Mary Anderson was taken
along, but died at about four o'clock on the morning of the 22d of
August. We had some chicken here, but no bread. Mary ate of the
chicken, and drank some of the broth. This was the last she ever ate. I
was with her when she died. It rained very hard a part of the night,
and the water ran through and under the tepee, on the ground, and
Mary was wet, and had no bed-clothing to keep her dry or warm. She
was very thirsty, calling for water all the time, but otherwise did not
complain, and said but very little. I watched while Mattie slept, and
she watched while I slept. I was awake when she died, and she
dropped away so gently that I thought she was asleep, until Mattie
told me she was dead.

The Hanging of Thirty-eight Indians

The result of the matter was that the order of the president [Lincoln]
was obeyed, and on the 26th of December, 1862, thirty-eight of the
condemned Indians were executed by hanging at Mankato, one having
been pardoned by the president. Contemporaneous history, or rather
public general knowledge of what actually took place, says that the
pardoned Indian was hanged and one of the others liberated by

From Charles E. Flandrau, Narrative of the Indian War of 1862–1864, and
Following Campaigns in Minnesota *(n.p., 1890?), p. 748.*

mistake. . . . The hanging of the thirty-eight was done on one gallows, constructed in a square form, capable of sustaining ten men on each side. They were placed upon a platform facing inwards, and dropped by the cutting of a rope all at one time. The execution was successful in all its details, and reflects credit on the ingenuity and engineering skill of Capt. Burt of Stillwater, who was intrusted with the construction of the deadly machine.

11 / Urban Revolution: The New York City Draft Riot of 1863

America's greatest urban riot was probably the anti-draft violence in New York City from July 13 to July 16, 1863. The total killed (1,000 est.) far exceeds the fatalities of other leading urban riots such as Pittsburgh in 1877, Watts in 1965, and Detroit in 1967. Triggered by the attempt to draft New Yorkers for service in the Union Army of the Civil War, the violence quickly escalated into a general urban uprising and ethnic war in which the lower-class laborers, chiefly Irish Catholic immigrants, streamed out of the slums and tenements in an inchoate ferocious onslaught upon the authorities and the police. Involved also was major racial violence as the Irish vented their frustration and anti-war sentiment in vicious attacks upon New York's sizable black population, with whom the Irish competed for jobs. Order was finally restored by federal regiments rushed to New York from the victorious battlefield of Gettysburg. The following selections deal with the second day, July 14, when the violence was savage and uncontrolled. The document reveals the twofold aspect of the riot as a full-scale urban revolution and as an anti-Negro pogrom.

The Police and the Military on the Attack

The military force that had accompanied the police, had formed on the avenue, about a block and a half above where the latter were stationed, while the detachment was clearing the houses. Two howitzers were placed in position commanding the avenue. Colonel O'Brien, of the Eleventh New York Volunteers, who was raising a regiment for the war, had gathered together, apparently on his own responsibility, about fifty men, and appearing on the field, from his superior rank,

From Joel T. Headley, The Great Riots of New York, 1712 to 1873 (*New York:* E. B. Treat, 1873), pp. 196–97, 206–9, 213–14, 223, 224–25.

assumed command. For a short time the rioters remained quiet, but as the police marched away, they suddenly awoke out of their apparent indifference. Maddened at the sight of the mangled bodies of their friends stretched on the pavement, and enraged at their defeat by the police, they now turned on the soldiers, and began to pelt them with stones and brick-bats. O'Brien rode up and down the centre of the street a few times, evidently thinking his fearless bearing would awe the mob. But they only jeered him, and finding the attack growing hotter and more determined, he finally gave the order to fire.

The howitzers belched forth on the crowd, the soldiers levelled their pieces, and the whistling of minie-balls was heard on every side. Men and women reeled and fell on the sidewalk and in the street. One woman, with her child in her arms, fell, pierced with a bullet. The utmost consternation followed. The crowd knew from sad experience that the police would use their clubs, but they seemed to think it hardly possible that the troops would fire point-blank into their midst. But the deadly effect of the fire convinced them of their error, and they began to jostle and crowd each other in the effort to get out of its range. In a few minutes the avenue was cleared of the living, when the wounded and dead were cared for by their friends.

The Hunting of the Blacks

All this time the fight was going on in every direction, while the fire-bells continually ringing increased the terror that every hour became more wide-spread. Especially was this true of the negro population. From the outset, they had felt they were to be objects of vengeance, and all day Monday and to-day those who could leave, fled into the country. They crowded the ferry-boats in every direction, fleeing for life. But old men and women, and poor families, were compelled to stay behind, and meet the fury of the mob, and to-day it became a regular hunt for them. A sight of one in the streets would call forth a halloo, as when a fox breaks cover, and away would dash a half a dozen men in pursuit. Sometimes a whole crowd streamed after with shouts and curses, that struck deadly terror to the heart of the fugitive. If overtaken, he was pounded to death at once; if he escaped into a negro house for safety, it was set on fire, and the inmates made to share a common fate. Deeds were done and sights witnessed that one would not have dreamed of, except among savage tribes.

At one time there lay at the corner of Twenty-seventh Street and Seventh Avenue the dead body of a negro, stripped nearly naked, and around it a collection of Irishmen, absolutely dancing or shouting like wild Indians. Sullivan and Roosevelt Streets are great negro quarters, and here a negro was afraid to be seen in the street. If in want of something from a grocery, he would carefully open the door, and look up and down to see if any one was watching, and then steal cautiously forth, and hurry home on his errand. Two boarding-houses here were surrounded by a mob, but the lodgers, seeing the coming storm fled. The desperadoes, finding only the owner left behind, wreaked their vengeance on him, and after beating him unmercifully, broke up the furniture, and then fired the buildings. A German store near by, because it was patronized extensively by negroes, shared the same fate, after its contents had been distributed among themselves. A negro barber's shop was next attacked, and the torch applied to it. A negro lodging-house in the same street next received the visit of these furies, and was soon a mass of ruins. Old men, seventy years of age, and young children, too young to comprehend what it all meant, were cruelly beaten and killed. The spirit of hell seemed to have entered the hearts of these men, and helpless womanhood was no protection against their rage.

Sometimes a stalwart negro would break away from his murderers, and run for his life. With no place of safety to which he could flee, he would be headed off in every direction, and forced towards the river. Driven at last to the end of a pier, he would leap off, preferring to take his chances in the water rather than among these bloody men. If bruised and beaten in his desperate struggle for life, he would soon sink exhausted with his efforts. Sometimes he would strike out for a ship, but more often dive under the piers, and hold on to a timber for safety, until his yelling pursuers had disappeared, when he would crawl stealthily out, and with terrified face peer in every direction to see if they had gone. Two were thus run off together into the East River. It was a strange spectacle to see a hundred Irishmen pour along the streets after a poor negro. If he could reach a police station he felt safe; but, alas! if the force happened to be away on duty, he could not stay even there. Whenever the police could strike the track of the mad hunt, they stopped it summarily, and the pursuers became the pursued, and received the punishment they had designed for the negro. All this was in the nineteenth century, and in the metropolis of the freest and most enlightened nation on earth.

The hunt for these poor creatures became so fearful, and the utter impossibility to protect them in their scattered localities so apparent, that they were received into the police stations. But these soon proved inadequate, and they were taken to head-quarters and the arsenal, where they could be protected against the mob. Here the poor creatures were gathered by hundreds, and slept on the floor, and were regularly fed by the authorities.

The Mob Out of Control

The riot had almost ceased to wear any political aspect since the attack on the *Tribune* office, the day before, had been defeated. An occasional shout or the sight of a negro might now and then remind one of its origin, but devastation and plunder were the great objects that urged on the excited masses. The sacking of Opdyke's house was done chiefly by a few youngsters, who were simply following the example set them the day before; while the burning of negro buildings, the chasing and killing of negroes, seemed to have only a remote connection with the draft, and was simply the indulgence of a hatred they were hitherto afraid to gratify. So the setting fire to the Weehawken ferry afterwards, could be made to grow out of politics only so far as a man who kept a liquor saloon there was a known Republican. This seemed a weak inducement to draw a crowd so far, when more distinguished victims were all around them.

It is more probable that some personal enemy of parties in the vicinity, finding the mob ready to follow any cry, led them thither; for one man seemed to be the leader, who mounted on a fine cavalry horse, and brandishing a sword, galloped backwards and forwards through the crowd, giving his orders like a field officer. Mobs springing up everywhere, and flowing together often apparently by accident, each pursuing a different object: one chasing negroes and firing their dwellings; others only sacking a house, and others still, wreaking their vengeance on station-houses, while scores, the moment they got loaded down with plunder, hastened away to conceal it—all showed that the original cause of the uprising had been forgotten. A strong uncertainty seemed at times to keep them swaying backwards and forwards, as though seeking a definite object, or waiting for an appointed signal to move, and then at some shout would rush for a building, a negro, or station-house.

The Fighting at the Barricades

Towards evening a mob assembled over in Ninth Avenue, and went to work with some system and forethought. Instead of wandering round, firing and plundering as the whim seized them, they began to throw up barricades, behind which they could rally when the military and police came to attack them. Indeed, the same thing had been done on the east side of the city; while railroads had been torn up, and stages stopped, to keep them from carrying policemen rapidly from one quarter to another. . . .

The commencement of barricades to obstruct the movements of the police and military, after the Parisian fashion, was a serious thing, and must be nipped in the bud; and Captain Walling, of the Twentieth Precinct, who had been busy in this part of the city all the afternoon in dispersing the mob, sent to head-quarters for a military force to help remove them. He also sent to General Sandford, at the arsenal, for a company of soldiers, which was promised, but never sent.

At six o'clock a force of regulars arrived from General Brown, and repaired to the Precinct station-house. Captain Slott, of the Twentieth Precinct, took command of the police force detailed to coöperate with the troops, but delayed action till the arrival of the company promised from the arsenal. Meanwhile, the rioters kept strengthening the barricades between Thirty-seventh and Forty-third Streets, in Eighth Avenue, by lashing carts, wagons, and telegraph poles together with wire stripped from the latter. The cross streets were also barricaded. Time passed on, and yet the bayonets of the expected reinforcement from the arsenal did not appear. The two commanding officers now began to grow anxious; it would not do to defer the attack till after dark, for such work as was before them required daylight. At length, as the sun stooped to the western horizon, it was resolved to wait no longer, and the order to move forward was given. As they approached the first barricade, by Thirty-seventh Street, a volley was poured into them from behind it, followed by stones and brick-bats.

The police now fell back to the left, and the regulars advancing, returned the fire. The rioters, however, stood their ground, and for a time nothing was heard but the rapid roll of musketry. But the steady, well-directed fire of the troops, at length began to tell on the mob, and they at last broke, and fled to the next barricade. The police then advanced, and tore down the barricade, when the whole force moved on to the next. Here the fight was renewed, but the close and rapid volley of the troops soon scattered the wretches, when this also was removed. They kept on in this way, till the last barricade was abandoned, when the uncovered crowd broke and fled in wild disorder. The soldiers pressed after, breaking up into squads, and chasing and firing into the disjointed fragments as they drifted down the various streets.

12 / The Montana Vigilantes, 1863–65

One of the deadliest (30 victims) and most famous of all American vigilante movements was that of the rough new mining camps of Virginia City, Nevada City, and Bannack, Montana Territory, from 1863 to 1865. The main work of the vigilante movement was the shattering of the gang of "road agents" headed by the wily Henry Plummer, who used his office of sheriff as a cover for his criminal conspiracy. A classic contemporary account of the movement by Thomas J. Dimsdale, a friend of the vigilantes, spread the fame of the Montana movement and popularized the term vigilante *in the American language. The selection below relates the origin of the vigilante movement and describes the confession of road agent Erastus (Red) Yager and his hanging along with G. W. Brown on January 4, 1864. An educated man and future superintendent of public instruction in Montana, Thomas Dimsdale was typical of the frontier leading men who supported and led vigilante movements. His deep loathing for the frontier riffraff and his strongly pro-vigilante sentiments make the account an impassioned one.*

Two sister towns—Virginia and Nevada—claim the honor of taking the first steps towards the formation of a Vigilance Committee. The truth is, that five men in Virginia and one in Nevada commenced simultaneously to take the initiative in the matter. Two days had not elapsed before their efforts were united, and when once a beginning had been made, the ramification of the league of safety and order extended, in a week or two, all over the Territory, and, on the 14th day of January, 1864, the *coup de grâce* was given to the power of the band by the execution of five of the chief villains, in Virginia City. The details of the rapid and masterly operations which occupied the few weeks immediately succeeding the execution of Ives, will appear in the following chapters.

The reasons why the organizations was so generally approved and so numerously and powerfully supported, were such as appealed to the simpathies of all men, who had anything to lose, or who thought their lives safer under the dominion of a body which, upon the whole, it must be admitted, has from the first acted with a wisdom, a justice and

From Thomas J. Dimsdale, The Vigilantes of Montana . . . *(Virginia City, Montana: Montana Post Press, 1866), pp. 104, 114–17.*

a vigor never surpassed on this continent, and rarely, if ever, equalled. Merchants, miners, mechanics and professional men, alike, joined in the movement, until, within an incredibly short space of time, the Road Agents and their friends were in a state of constant and well grounded fear, lest any remarks they might make confidentially to an acquaintance might be addressed to one who was a member of the much dreaded Committee. . . .

The culprits were informed that they should be taken to Virginia, and were given in charge to a trustworthy and gallant man, with a detachment of seven, selected from the whole troop. This escort reached Lorraine's in two hours. The rest of the men arrived at sun down. The prisoners were given up, and the leader of the little party, who had not slept for four or five nights, lay down to snatch a brief, but welcome repose. About 10 P.M., he was awakened, and the significant, "We want you," announced "business."

The tone and manner of the summons at once dispelled even his profound and sorely needed slumber. He rose without further parley and went from the parlor to the bar-room where Red and Brown were lying in a corner, asleep. Red got up at the sound of his footsteps, and said, "You have treated me like a gentleman, and I know I am going to die—I am going to be hanged." "Indeed," said his quondam custodian, "that's pretty rough." In spite of a sense of duty, he felt what he said deeply. "It is pretty rough," continued Yager, "but I merited this, years ago. What I want to say is that I know all about the gang, and there are men in it that deserve this more than I do; but I should die happy if I could see them hanged, or know that it would be done. I don't say this to get off. I don't want to get off." He was told that it would be better if he should give all the information in his possession, if only for the sake of his kind. Times had been very hard, and "you know, Red," said the Vigilanter, "that men have been shot down in broad day light —not for money, or even for hatred, but for LUCK, and it must be put a stop to."

To this he assented, and the captain being called, all that had passed was stated to him. He said that the prisoner had better begin at once, and his words should be taken down. Red began by informing them that Plummer was chief of the band; Bill Bunton second in command and stool pigeon; Sam Bunton, roadster, (sent away for being a drunkard;) Cyrus Skinner, roadster, fence and spy. At Virginia City, George Ives, Steven Marshland, Dutch John (Wagner,) Aleck Carter, Whiskey Bill, (Graves,) were roadsters; Geo. Shears was a roadster and horse-thief; Johnny Cooper and Buck Stinson were also roadsters; Ned Ray was council-room keeper at Bannack City; Mexican Frank and Bob Zachary were also roadsters; Frank Parish was roadster and horse-thief; Boon Helm and Club-Foot George were roadsters; Haze Lyons and Bill Hunter were roadsters and telegraph men; George Lowry, Billy Page, Doc Howard, Jem Romaine, Billy Terwilliger and Gad Moore were roadsters. The pass-word was "Innocent." They wore a necktie fastened with a "sailor's knot," and shaved down to moustache and chin whiskers. He admitted that he was one of the gang; but denied—as they invariably did—that he was a murderer. He also stated that Brown—his fellow captive—acted in the capacity before mentioned.

He spoke of Bill Bunton with a fierece animosity quite unlike his usual suave and courteous manner. To him, he said, he owed his present miserable position. He it was that first seduced him to commit crime, at Lewiston. He gave the particulars of the robberies of the coaches and of many other crimes, naming the perpetrators. As these details have been already supplied or will appear in the course of the narrative, they are omitted, in order to avoid a useless repetition.

After serious reflection, it had been decided that the two culprits should be executed forthwith, and the dread preparations were immediately made for carrying out the resolution.

The trial of George Ives had demonstrated most unquestionably that no amount of certified guilt was sufficient to enlist popular sympathy exclusively on the side of justice, or to render the just man other than a mark for vengeance. The majority of men sympathize, in spite of the voice of reason, with the murderers instead of the victims; a course of conduct which appears to us inexplicable, though we know it to be common. Every fibre of our frame vibrates with anger and disgust when we meet a ruffian, a murderer or a marauder. Mawkish sentimentalism we abhor. The thought of murdered victims, dishonored females, plundered wayfarers, burning houses, and the rest of the sad evidences of villainy, completely excludes mercy from our view. Honor, truth and the sacrifice of self to considerations of justice and the good of mankind—these claim, we had almost said our adoration; but for the low, brutal, cruel, lazy, ignorant, insolent, sensual and blasphemous miscreants that infest the frontiers, we entertain but one sentiment—aversion—deep, strong, and unchangeable. For such cases, the rope is the only prescription that avails as a remedy. But, though such feelings must be excited in the minds of good citizens, when brought face to face with such monsters as Stinson, Helm, Gallagher, Ives, Skinner, or Graves, the calm courage and penitent conduct of

Erastus Yager have the opposite effect, and the loss of the goodly vessel thus wrecked forever, must inspire sorrow, though it may not and ought not to disarm justice.

Brief were the preparations needed. A lantarn [*sic*] and some stools were brought from the house, and the party, crossing the creek behind Lorraine's Ranch, made for the trees that still bear the marks of the axe which trimmed off the superfluous branches. On the road to the gallows, Red was cool, calm and collected. Brown sobbed and cried for mercy, and prayed God to take care of his wife and family in Minnesota. He was married to a squaw. Red, overhearing him, said, sadly but firmly, "Brown, if you had thought of this three years ago, you would not be here now, or give these boys this trouble."

After arriving at the fatal trees, they were pinioned and stepped on to the stools, which had been placed one on the other to form a drop. Brown and the man who was adjusting the rope, tottered and fell into the snow; but recovering himself quickly, the Vigilanter said quietly, "Brown we must do better than that."

Brown's last words were, "God Almighty save my soul."

The frail platform flew from under him, and his life passed away almost with the twang of the rope.

Red saw his comrade drop; but no sign of trepidation was visible. His voice was as calm and quiet as if he had been conversing with old friends. He said he knew that he should be followed and hanged when he met the party on the Divide. He wished that they would chain him and carry him along to where the rest were, that he might see them punished. Just before he was launched into eternity, he asked to shake hands with them all, which having done, he begged of the man who had escorted him to Lorraine's, that he would follow and punish the rest. The answer was given in these words, "Red we will do it, if there's any such thing in the book." The pledge was kept.

His last words were, "Good bye, boys; God bless you. You are on a good undertaking." The frail footing on which he stood gave way, and this dauntless and yet guilty criminal died without a struggle. It was pitiful to see one whom nature intended for a hero, dying—and that justly—like a dog.

A label was pinioned to his back bearing the legend:

"Red! Road Agent and Messenger."

The inscription on the paper fastened on to Brown's clothes was:

"Brown! Corresponding Secretary."

The fatal trees still smile as they don the green livery of Spring, or wave joyfully in the Summer breeze; but when the chill blast of winter moans over the snow-clad prairie, the wind sighing and creaking through the swaying boughs seems, to the excited listener, to be still laden with the sighs and sounds of that fatal night. *Fiat Justitia ruat cælum.*

The bodies were left suspended, and remained so for some days before they were buried. The ministers of justice expected a battle on their arrival at Nevada; but they found the Vigilantes organized in full force, and each man, as he uncocked his gun and dismounted, heaved a deep sigh of relief. The crisis was past.

13 / Indians Slaughtered by Whites: The Sand Creek Massacre of 1864

Three years of savage raids by the Cheyenne and Arapaho had goaded Colorado settlers into a vengeful frenzy. Finally, in November 1864, Colonel J. M. Chivington led a force of 1,000 militia against the Indians. Believing the war had been settled, Chief Black Kettle and 500 Indians were peacefully sleeping in a camp on Sand Creek, where at dawn on November 28 the militia struck. The result was the brutal slaughter of nearly all of the men, women, and children in the camp. The account of the massacre which follows is by Robert Bent, half-Indian and half-white, who acted as a guide for Chivington. Bent's relation attests the sort of barbarity that was the norm in fighting between whites and Indians.

I am twenty-four years old; was born on the Arkansas river. I am pretty well acquainted with the Indians of the plains, having spent most of my life among them. I was employed as guide and interpreter at Fort Lyon by Major Anthony. Colonel Chivington ordered me to accompany him on his way to Sand creek. The command consisted of from nine hundred to one thousand men, principally Colorado volunteers. We left Fort Lyon at eight o'clock in the evening, and came on to the Indian camp at daylight the next morning. Colonel Chivington surrounded the village with his troops. When we came in sight of the camp I saw the American flag waving and heard Black Kettle

U.S. *Congress,* Condition of the Indian Tribes: Report of the Joint Special Committee, appointed under Joint Resolution of March 3, 1865 (*Washington: Government Printing Office, 1867*), *pp.* 95–96.

tell the Indians to stand round the flag, and there they were huddled—men, women, and children. This was when we were within fifty yards of the Indians. I also saw a white flag raised. These flags were in so conspicuous a position that they must have been seen. When the troops fired the Indians ran, some of the men into their lodges, probably to get their arms. They had time to get away if they had wanted to. I remained on the field five hours, and when I left there were shots being fired up the creek. I think there were six hundred Indians in all. I think there were thirty-five braves and some old men, about sixty in all. All fought well. At the time the rest of the men were away from camp, hunting.

I visited the battle-ground one month afterwards; saw the remains of a good many; counted sixty-nine, but a number had been eaten by the wolves and dogs. After the firing the warriors put the squaws and children together, and surrounded them to protect them. I saw five squaws under a bank for shelter. When the troops came up to them they ran out and showed their persons to let the soldiers know they were squaws and begged for mercy, but the soldiers shot them all. I saw one squaw lying on the bank whose leg had been broken by a shell; a soldier came up to her with a drawn sabre; she raised her arm to protect herself, when he struck, breaking her arm; she rolled over and raised her other arm, when he struck, breaking it, and then left her without killing her. There seemed to be an indiscriminate slaughter of men, women, and children. There were some thirty or forty squaws collected in a hole for protection; they sent out a little girl about six years old with a white flag on a stick; she had not proceeded but a few steps when she was shot and killed. All the squaws in that hole were afterwards killed, and four or five bucks outside. The squaws offered no resistance. Every one I saw dead was scalped. I saw one squaw cut open with an unborn child, as I thought, lying by her side. Captain Soulé afterwards told me that such was the fact. I saw the body of White Antelope with the privates cut off, and I heard a soldier say he was going to make a tobacco-pouch out of them. I saw one squaw whose privates had been cut out.

I heard Colonel Chivington say to the soldiers as they charged past him, "Remember our wives and children murdered on the Platte and Arkansas." He occupied a position where he could not have failed to have seen the American flag, which I think was a garrison flag, six by twelve. He was within fifty yards when he planted his battery. I saw a little girl about five years of age who had been hid in the sand; two soldiers discovered her, drew their pistols and shot her, and then pulled her out of the sand by the arm. I saw quite a number of infants in arms killed with their mothers. There were trading in the village at the time John Smith, a soldier named Louderback, and a teamster of young Colley's named Clark. They were trading goods said to belong to Dexter Colley and John Smith. The goods traded were similar to those they had been in the habit of trading before. I have heard the Indians charge Major Colley with trading their own goods to them.

14 / John Wesley Hardin of Texas: Peerless Gunman, 1868–75

The greatest of all Western gunmen was John Wesley Hardin of Texas. In a seven-year period he killed more than 20 men—more than Billy the Kid or Jesse James, both of whom surpassed him in notoriety. Hardin never killed for money and, although often a fugitive from justice, was not a criminal in the usual sense of the word. Rather, as a killer he was the product of his place and time. The son of a Methodist minister, Hardin was born in 1856. He grew up in the violent region of central Texas and as a youth was ardently pro-Southern and anti-Negro. He fell into his death-dealing career not from any design but as a result of the racial, political, and family-feud tensions that converged upon him in the turbulent Reconstruction era of Texas. As time passed, pride in his prowess as a killer set in, and he never avoided a fight. At his death Hardin left behind a manuscript of his autobiography, which subsequently became a classic in the history of Western violence. The following selections are from Hardin's autobiography. They recount his first killing at the age of 15; the gunplay with which as a boy of 18 he dazzled and awed Wild Bill Hickock in Abilene, Kansas; and his lightning fast shooting of Deputy Sheriff Charles Webb in Comanche, Texas, in 1874. By 1895, after a long 16-year prison term, Hardin, at the age of 42, had lost his touch and was shot from behind in an El Paso saloon by a medium-grade Texas gunman, John Selman.

Hardin's First Victim, The Negro Mage

In the fall of 1868, I went down to my uncle's (Barnett Hardin) in Polk county, about four miles north of Livingstone. I was in the

From *John Wesley Hardin*, The Life of John Wesley Hardin as Written by Himself (*Seguin, Texas: Smith and Moore, 1896*), pp. 11–13, 44–45, 89–93.

habit of making these trips, though I was then but 15 years old. This time they were making sugar and I took the trip to see them, carrying my pistol of course. I met a negro named Mage close to Moscow who had belonged to Judge Houlshousen, a brother to my Uncle Barnett Hardin's wife. I had a cousin named Barnett Jones who matched himself and me against this Moscow negro in a wrestling bout. The negro was a large, powerful man, and we were but two boys. Nevertheless we threw him down the first fall. He was not satisfied, so we threw him again, and this time scratched his face a little and made it bleed. Negro like, he got mad and said he could whip me and would do it. Barnett and others standing around stopped us from fighting. This seemed to make Mage all the more angry. He said he would kill me, and went after his gun. I went up to the house to get mine, too, but Uncle Barnett got on to the game and made me stay in the house, while that negro went around cursing and abusing me, saying "that he would kill me or die himself; that no white boy could draw his blood and live; that a bird never flew too high not to come to the ground." Uncle Barnett then took a hand and ordered Mage off the plantation. [The next day Hardin encountered Mage.]

I stopped in the road and he came at me with his big stick. He struck me, and as he did it I pulled out a Colt's 44 six-shooter and told him to get back. By this time he had my horse by the bridle, but I shot him loose. He kept coming back and every time he would start I would shoot again and again until I shot him down. I went to Uncle Clabe Houlshousen and brought him and another man back to where Mage was lying. Mage still showed fight and called me a liar. If it had not been for my uncle I would have shot him again. Uncle Houlshousen gave me a $20 gold piece and told me to go home and tell father all about the big fight; that Mage was bound to die, and for me to look out for the Yankee soldiers who were all over the country at that time. Texas like other states, was then overrun with carpet-baggers and bureau agents who had the United States Army to back them up in their meanness. Mage shortly died in November, 1868. This was the first man I ever killed, and it nearly distracted my father and mother when I told them.

Hardin Faces Down Wild Bill Hickock in Abilene, Kansas, 1871

I spent most of my time in Abilene in the saloons and gambling houses, playing poker, faro, and seven-up. One day I was rolling ten pins and my best horse was hitched outside in front of the saloon. I had two six-shooters on and of course I knew the saloon people would raise a row if I did not pull them off. Several Texans were there rolling ten pins and drinking. I suppose we were pretty noisy. Wild Bill came in and said we were making too much noise and told me to pull off my pistols until I got ready to go out of town. I told him I was ready to go now, but did not propose to put up my pistols, go or no go. He went out and I followed him. I started up the street when someone behind me shouted out: "Set up. All down but mine."

Wild Bill whirled around and met me. He said: "What are you howling about, and what are you doing with those pistols on."

I said: "I am just taking in the town."

He pulled his pistol and said: "Take those pistols off. I arrest you."

I said all right and pulled them out of the scabbard, but while he was reaching for them I reversed them and whirled them over on him with the muzzles in his face, springing back at the same time. I told him to put his pistols up, which he did. I cursed him for a long haired scoundrel that would shoot a boy with his back to him (as I had been told he intended to do me). He said, "Little Arkansaw, you have been wrongly informed." . . .

I shouted: "This is my fight and I'll kill the first man that fires a gun."

Bill said: "You are the gamest and quickest boy I ever saw. Let us compromise this matter and I will be your friend. Let us go in here and take a drink, as I want to talk to you and give you some advice."

At first I thought he might be trying to get the drop on me, but he finally convinced me of his good intentions and we went in and took a drink. We went into a private room and I had a long talk with him and we came out friends.

The Killing of Charles Webb
in Comanche, Texas, 1874

I had heard that morning that Charles Webb, the deputy sheriff from Brown county, had come over to Comanche with fifteen men to kill me and capture Jim Taylor for the reward. I also heard that he had said that John Karnes, the sheriff of Comanche, was no man or sheriff because he allowed a set of murderers to stay around him, headed by the notorious John Wesley Hardin, and as he (Karnes) would not attend to his business, he would do it for him. I knew that Webb had arrested a whole cow camp a short time before and had treated a man whom he called John Wesley Hardin most cruelly, telling him he was afraid of his own name and jobbed him in the side with his gun, knowing positively that I was not in the country at that time. If I had been there I would have taught him a lesson sooner.

He did not make any breaks at the race tracks, but when we all came back to town he swore time and time again that he would kill me and capture Jim Taylor, and that this would be done before the sun went down. When I was told this I laughed and said I hoped he would put it off till dark or altogether. [Later in the day Hardin stood in front of a saloon talking to friends.]

About this time Dave Karnes remarked: "Here comes that damned Brown County sheriff."

I turned around and faced the man whom I had seen coming up the street. He had on six-shooters and was in about fifteen steps from me, advancing. He stopped when he got to within five steps of me, then stopped and scrutinized me closely, with his hands behind him. I asked him: "Have you any papers for my arrest."

He said: "I don't know you."

I said: "My name is John Wesley Hardin."

He said: "Now I know you, but have no papers for your arrest."

"Well," said I, "I have been informed that the sheriff of Brown county has said that Sheriff Karnes of this county was no sheriff or he would not allow me to stay around Comanche with my murdering pals."

He said: "I am not responsible for what the sheriff of Brown county says. I am only a deputy."

So Dave Karnes spoke up and said: "Men, there can be no difference between you about John Karnes," and said: "Mr. Webb, let me introduce you to Mr. Hardin."

I asked him what he had in his hand behind his back, and he showed a cigar. I said: "Mr. Webb, we were just going to take a drink or a cigar; won't you join us?"

He replied, "certainly." As I turned around to go in the north door, I heard some one say, "Look out, Jack." It was Bud Dixon, and as I turned around I saw Charles Webb drawing his pistol. He was in the act of presenting it when I jumped to one side, drew my pistol and fired.

In the meantime Webb had fired, hitting me in the left side, cutting the length of it, inflicting an ugly and painful wound. My aim was good and a bullet hole in the left cheek did the work. He fell against the wall and as he fell he fired a second shot, which went into the air.

In the meantime, my friends, Jim Taylor and Bud Dixon, seeing that Webb had taken the drop on me and had shot me, pulled their pistols and fired on him as he was falling, not knowing that I had killed him. Each shot hit him in the side and breast.

15 / Ku Klux Klan Violence in Mississippi, 1871

For more than 100 years Ku Klux Klan violence has plagued the nation and particularly the South. There have been three Ku Klux Klans: the first, of Reconstruction times (1865–71), the second, of the 1920s (a nationwide organization), and the third, of the 1950s and 1960s (restricted, largely, to the South). The documents that follow illustrate the violence of the first Ku Klux Klan, the movement that served as the prototype and inspiration for the later Klans. Founded in 1865, the first Klan had its most active years from 1867 to 1871. It aimed to undermine Reconstruction in the former Confederate states by using violence to intimidate white Radical Republican politicians and officials and to reduce black people to a state of abject subordination to Southern whites. The belt of Klan terror stretched from the Carolinas and Florida to Arkansas. A similar movement, the Knights of the White Camelia, dominated the Gulf Coast region. The selections below reveal the nature of Klan violence and intimidation in northeastern Mississippi in 1871. They are typical of the movement as a whole.

The Whipping of a Black Man

Columbus, Mississippi, November 11, 1871.

Joseph Turner (colored) sworn and examined.

By the Chairman:

QUESTION: Where do you live?

ANSWER: I live here in town.

QUESTION: State to the committee whether you have ever been visited and whipped by the Ku-Klux in this county.

ANSWER: Yes, sir; I have.

QUESTION: Was it near Caledonia?

ANSWER: Yes, sir.

QUESTION: How long ago was it?

U.S. Congress, Testimony Taken by the Joint Select Committee to Inquire into the Condition of Affairs in the Late Insurrectionary States: Mississippi *(Washington: Government Printing Office, 1872), pp. 271–73, 286, 769–71.*

ANSWER: It has been, as nigh as I can remember, three weeks before the court sat in Oxford in the summer.

QUESTION: Were you at your house at the time?

ANSWER: No, sir; at my sister's house.

QUESTION: What time in the night did they visit you?

ANSWER: About 11 o'clock.

QUESTION: Were you in bed?

ANSWER: No, sir.

QUESTION: State the circumstances, and how many men were concerned.

ANSWER: There was ten men that came in the yard; and there was, as nigh as I could get at it, it looked like the crowd was twenty; they did not come in; they stopped down in the lane in the road. When they first came in I was sitting down; the door was standing open; I saw them before they got to the house, but I was not afeard; I knew very well that they were going to ride that night. . . .

QUESTION: How long after you got to your sister's before they came?

ANSWER: About three-quarters of an hour, as nigh as I can get at it.

QUESTION: What did they do?

ANSWER: They came up there; I saw them coming before they got to the house, and I said, "Here comes the Ku-Klux," and everybody sat still in the house. I thought they were going on by, there was so many of them; the front part of them went on by, but there was ten men got down off of the horses and hitched the horses at the fence, and they came up and asked for Joe Turner. I said, "He is here." They said, "Tell him to come out; we want to talk to him." I would not come out. Two men came in, and caught me by the waistband of my pants on each side and took me out. Both of them had a pistol in his hand, and one before me with a pistol; and they carried me up the road, and another one spoke sitting on a horse; and they brought me down the road like they were going to the bottom. They took me about a hundred yards, to a little pine bush by the roadside, and there they whipped me.

QUESTION: How many whipped you?

ANSWER: Only one.

QUESTION: How many licks?

ANSWER: He gave me fifty licks with a concern—a half switch and half stick—and they struck me five licks with a stick—two licks on each arm. To keep the licks off, I put up my arms, and they killed my arms dead, and they struck me one over the head. It was six weeks before I could grab anything in my hand.

QUESTION: What did they say they whipped you for?

ANSWER: They said they heard I was carrying a pistol to shoot the Ku-Klux with. I had one, but it was not that long, [illustrating;] a little pocket-pistol. I only paid seventy-five cents for it. I could not hit a man across this house. I did not have it at the house with me; it was at the shop. . . .

QUESTION: Were their horses disguised?

ANSWER: The horses were half covered, back to the saddle; the head and neck were covered.

QUESTION: What kind of disguise did the men have on?

ANSWER: White, with horns on their heads, and then they had belts around them—leather belts, and pistols stuck down outside, and most every one had a stick about a foot and a half long, with a string in it to the wrist.

QUESTION: Did you hear any of the Ku-Klux whistle?

ANSWER: Yes, sir; they were whistling when they came there, making all kinds of fuss—some hollering like owls, some whippoorwills, and some talked talk I could not understand. They talked while they were getting me out of the house in broken language; and after they got outside, where they whipped me, they all got in a row, and asked me did I know any of them.

QUESTION: Did they talk in natural voices?

ANSWER: They talked in natural voices after they got me out of the house. They asked me if I knew any of them. I knew them, but I did not dare own it for fear they would kill me.

QUESTION: You say when they were trying to get you out of the house they disguised their voices?

ANSWER: Yes, sir; they talked like they were Irishmen, or something —talked broken language.

QUESTION: Did you know any of the men by their voices or size?

ANSWER: Yes, sir; some of the men I worked with; I knew them by their horses and by their voices.

QUESTION: Were they some of the same men you had seen at the store that night?

ANSWER: Yes, sir; they were some of the same men; and the man that done the whipping, he as good as said that he intended to do it. I worked with him three months in the year. I was not making anything. I was only getting $10 a month and feeding my family, and I could not make anything; and I told him I could not make anything and I quit; and he told me when I went away from his house that if I left there I had better go farther than Columbus. I told him I would go to Columbus, where I moved from. He told me I had better go farther than Columbus; I had better go clear out of his reach.

QUESTION: Had you been working on his plantation?

ANSWER: Yes; better than three months.

QUESTION: What is his name?

ANSWER: John Stinson.

QUESTION: What other men did you recognize?

ANSWER: There was John Stinson, Will Stinson, (his brother,) Jess Stinson—he was old man Andy Stinson's son—and then there was one Gardner; he is a merchant there; and there was Laney Williams; there was John Kidd and his son John; and there was Fullen Wiler and Jasper Webb.

The Whipping of the Federal District Tax Assessor

QUESTION: State the transaction fully; begin and give us the whole of it.

ANSWER: I was warned during the day of the 9th that the Ku-Klux had been riding the night before for me. It was very stormy, and the wind was very high, and it had rained very hard on the night of the 8th. A colored man, knowing that I was there, came to me the next day and told me that some Ku-Klux had been out, and that some colored men had seen them; that they had been at Mark Troup's place, where they had understood I was to stay. The colored men asked me to go out of the country, for they knew that the Ku-Klux would get me if they could. I laughed at their fears, and had no idea that they would attack a United States officer. During the day I attended to my duties; and at 9 o'clock that night I was in bed at Mr. Ross's house. At 10 o'clock I was awakened by a loud call out of doors upon Mr. Ross for "the man who was in the house." I stepped to my window, which was on the ground floor, and saw that the premises were completely covered with men dressed in white; I knew then I was with the Ku-Klux. . . .

QUESTION: They were civil in their manner?

ANSWER: Yes, sir; they were civil. One of them commenced to curse; he began, "God damn," and was going to say something, when the captain stopped him, and said that he should not do that; that all they wanted of me was to get me out of the country; they said they did not like my radical ways anyway. I asked them if their operations were against the radical party; they said they were; that they had suffered and endured the radical sway as long as they could; that the radicals had oppressed them with taxation; that they were oppressing them all the time, and that I was the instrument of collecting the taxes; that they had stood it just as long as they could, and that this was their way of getting rid of it; that they were bound to rid themselves of radicals, or else kill them, or if it took the killing of them, or something to that effect. There was a colored school and a white school in the neighborhood. I knew most of the men there were from that neighborhood; I asked them with reference to Mr. Davis's school; that was the white school, where I supposed the most of their children were attending; I asked them if they were not satisfied with his school; they said, "No"; that they liked Davis well enough as a teacher, but that they were opposed to the free-school system entirely; that the whites could do as they had always done before; that they could educate their own children; that so far as the negroes were concerned, they did not need educating, only to work. They said they had no objection to Davis at all, but that they could manage their own affairs without the State or the United States sending such as I was there to educate their children, and at the same time to educate the negroes too. After the conversation on the school subject closed, one of them said, "Well, sir, what do you say to our warning? Will you leave?" I told them I should leave Monroe County at my pleasure, and not until I got ready. . . .

. . . They ordered me to take off my coat, which I refused to do; they then took it off by force. After that they asked if I consented to leave, and I still refused. They said that if I would promise them, I should go back to my bed and sleep quietly, and they would all go on home; they really urged in every way that it was possible for men to do to get me to promise to leave the county and the State without any violence. They then showed me a rope with a noose, and said that was for such as myself who were stubborn; that if I did not consent to leave I should die, that dead men told no tales. At this time I saw a man coming from toward the horses, from where I then supposed, and where I afterward knew the horses were; he had a stirrup-strap some inch and a quarter in width, and at least an eighth of an inch thick; it was very stout leather; the stirrup was a wooden one. As he came up he threw down the wooden stirrup and came on toward me, and I saw that he was intending to hit me with the strap, that that was the weapon they intended to use first. He came on, and without further ceremony at all—I was in my shirt sleeves—he struck me two blows, calling out, "One, two," and said, "Now, boys, count." They counted every lash they gave me. The first man gave me ten blows himself, standing on my left side, striking over my left arm and on my back; the next one gave me five blows. Then a fresh hand took it and gave me ten blows; that made twenty-five. They then stopped, and asked me again if I would leave the county. I still refused, and told them that now they had commenced they could go just as far as they pleased; that all had been done that I cared for; that I would as soon die then as to take what I had taken. They continued to strike their blows on my back in the same way until they had reached fifty. None of them struck more than ten blows, some of them only three, and some as low as two. They said they all wanted to get a chance at me; that I was stubborn, and just such a man as they liked to pound. When they had struck me fifty blows they stopped again and asked me if I would leave; I told them I would not. Then one of the strongest and most burly in the crowd took the strap himself and gave me twenty-five blows without stopping; that made seventy-five; I heard them say, "Seventy-five." At that time my strength gave way entirely; I grew dizzy and cold; I asked for my coat; that is the last I remember for several minutes. When I recovered myself they were still about me; I was standing; I do not think I had been down; they must have held me up all the time. I heard them say, "He is not dead yet; he is a live man yet; dead men tell no tales." But still they all seemed disposed, as I thought, to let me go; I heard no threatening, except what passed a few moments afterward. They all passed in front of me, or a great number of them—I will not say all—and drew their pistols and showed them to me; they told me that if I was not gone within ten days they were all sworn in their camp, and sworn positively, that they would kill me, either privately or publicly. . . .

QUESTION: What is the state of mind among the colored people, among the republicans, both white and black, but especially among the colored people, which is produced by these operations?

ANSWER: The excitement was the most intense I have ever seen under any circumstances. The demoralization among the colored people was perfect. We have very few white republicans there; most of the republicans are colored people. The excitement reached the distressing point. I never in my life saw so high an excitement in any other place as there was on the 8th and 9th of March, when I was in the neighborhood where these murders had been committed.

QUESTION: Was the excitement which was among the colored people mainly the excitement of fear?

ANSWER: The most abject fear; they dared not even go to town.

16 / Terrorism in the Hard Coal Country: The Molly Maguires, 1862–78

For 15 years a terrorist organization of Irish miners flourished in the anthracite (hard coal) field of Schuylkill and Carbon counties in northeastern Pennsylvania. Outside the area the Ancient Order of Hibernians was a respectable, though secret, benevolent and social society of Irish Catholics. But in the anthracite region economic and ethnic tensions put the Ancient Order of Hibernians under the domination of its terrorist inner circle, who called themselves the "Molly Maguires." In Ireland there had been a Molly Maguire tradition of anti-British violence that was brought to this country by the Irish immigrant miners.

The Molly Maguires in America reserved the bulk of their murders, assaults, and destruction of property for the native American or English mine owners and bosses who oppressed the Irish miners with low wages, long hours, and squalid living and working conditions. Protestant-Catholic tensions also figured in the troubles, as well as the usual Irish-English hostility. The Catholic Church strongly opposed the Molly Maguires but exerted little control over the bitter and hotheaded miners and their supporters.

Body-Masters and Murder Plans

The local unit of the Ancient Order of Hibernians was the division. The head of each division was the body-master, who also functioned as the leader of the terrorist inner circle of Molly Maguires. The system of trading off murder assignments among various units, described below, has been typical of criminal and terrorist organizations in both Europe and America.

Among the Mollie Maguires there is a thoroughly arranged system for the commission of crimes. A member having made complaint of

From James D. McCabe [Edward W. Martin, pseud.], The History of the Great Riots . . . (Philadelphia: National Publishing Company, 1877), pp. 489–90, 500–501.

certain parties who have offended him, or who are considered dangerous to the order, the matter is referred to the body-master, or a meeting of the division, or to a meeting of the body-masters of all the di-
visions and other leading men of the order, called by the county
delegate. The body-master or the meeting decides whether any action
shall be taken in the premises, and what shall be the nature of the
punishment. In case punishment is decided upon, application is made
either to the county delegate or to the body-master of another division
for men to commit the outrage, the men furnished being always unknown to the victim or victims. A solemn promise is given that the
favor will be returned by the division needing the service, whenever
called upon by the other. The body-master of the division called upon
either directly appoints the men, or they are selected by lot. A member refusing to obey the orders of his body-master on such an occasion
is expelled from the order. The men, having been selected, are despatched to the head-quarters of the division needing them, and are
placed upon the track of their victims as soon as possible. They are
required either to kill or brutally beat the persons pointed out to them,
or to burn certain houses or mining structures.

The person committing the crime is in nine cases out of ten a
stranger to his victim, and is actuated by no personal ill will to him.
He simply obeys the orders of his society, and murders or burns in
cold blood, and with a deliberation that is appalling. Murder is the
most common form of punishment with the Mollies. "Dead men tell
no tales," is the principle of the order. It is enough for a man to incur
the dislike of an influential member of the order to forfeit his life.
The murder is generally committed in some lonely place, and with
all the aggravated features of assassination. Though the conduct of
the murderers is in the highest degree cowardly, they are regarded as
heroes by the Mollies, and large rewards have been paid by the society
for the killing of particularly obnoxious individuals. Should a member
commit murder or a robbery on his individual account, the act is
indorsed by the society, and its whole influence is used to screen and
protect the criminal.

The Murder of John P. Jones, September 3, 1875

*Mine foreman John P. Jones had angered the Molly Maguires by
blacklisting one of their members. The way in which the Mollies
wreaked fatal vengeance on Jones was typical of their assassinations,
although it was the last of the sensational murders by the Mollies.
James McParlan (mentioned in the account below under his alias,*

James McKenna), a Pinkerton detective, had infiltrated the Molly Maguires; his crucial disclosures in a series of trials led to the hanging of 20 Molly Maguires and the imprisoning of others in 1877–78. Thus came to an end Molly Maguireism.

In the meantime the demand had been made by the Coaldale Mollies for men to kill John P. Jones, and a meeting of the Shenandoah division was held on the night of the 1st of September, at the house of Frank McAndrew, the body-master, to select the murderers. Thomas Munley and Michael Darcy volunteered for the work, and John McGrail and James McKenna were appointed by the body-master. McKenna had sought the appointment in the hope of preventing the murder. He did succeed in delaying the starting of his companions, and as he was congratulating himself that Jones would have time to get out of the way, news came that he had been murdered by another band of Mollies.

It seems that he had given offence to some of the Mollies of the Mount Laffee division (near Pottsville), and the body-master of that division, Jerry Kane, had appointed Edward Kelly and another man to do the work. As the other was a married man, a young man named Michael J. Doyle volunteered to take his place, and the offer was accepted. They went to Tamaqua on the 1st of September, bearing a letter of introduction to Thomas Carroll. Carroll sent them in charge of James Kerrigan to Alexander Campbell at Storm Hill. Kerrigan introduced his companions to Campbell as the men sent over to kill Jones, and they were warmly greeted by Campbell.

Campbell took them up to McGeehan's saloon on Summit Hill, and introduced them to that murderer. Pistols were carefully selected, and as neither Kerrigan, Doyle nor Kelly knew John P. Jones, Campbell carefully described his personal appearance to them. They spent the night and next day and night in seeking opportunities to kill their victim, but without success.

On the morning of the 3d John P. Jones, who had on the previous night slept at his house at Storm Hill, for the first time in many months, left home and started for the office of the general superintendent near the Landsford depot. The train from Tamaqua was nearly due, and about one hundred persons were awaiting it at the depot. Just as Jones approached the depot, he was suddenly confronted by Kelly and Doyle, who fired rapidly at him, lodging several balls in his body. He fell dead, and the murderers under the guidance of Kerrigan fled.

17 / A Family Feud: The Hatfields versus the McCoys, 1873–88

A well-known feature of American life in the late nineteenth century was the violent family feud. Among many lethal feuds in the southwest were the 30-year-long Sutton-Taylor feud (1869–99) of Texas and the Graham-Tewksbury feud (1886–92) of Arizona, which raged until all but one member of the two families had perished. The region best known for family feuds was the southern Appalachians, especially Kentucky and West Virginia. Here the many murderous vendettas included the Martin-Tolliver (1884–87) and the Hargis-Cockrell (1902–03) feuds of eastern Kentucky and the one that has become a part of the nation's legend and lore—the Hatfield-McCoy feud, which took nearly a score of lives along the Kentucky-West Virginia border. Enmity between the two families smoldered after the Civil War, burst into full flame from 1873 to 1888, and did not entirely subside until years later. The following selections are by T. C. Crawford, a New York journalist who visited the isolated mountainous feud region and interviewed the patriarchal William Anderson (Devil Anse) Hatfield. In Crawford's book he is called Ance Hatfield.

Hatfields, McCoys, and the Killings of 1882

The Hatfield and McCoy families are the two leading mountain families of their region. The Hatfields live on the east side of the Tug River in West Virginia. The McCoys live in Pike County, Ky., on the other side of the river. These two families own large tracts of land and are thoroughly well-to-do. Neither of the heads of the families reads nor writes. Some of the children now growing up have the rudiments of an ordinary education. The two families have had very close relations at different times by marriage and through business relations. During the war there were organized on both sides of the river what were known as "home guards."

These home guards were organized ostensibly for the protection of the property interests of their region against an invading foe, but instead of becoming a real home defense, they invariably followed the practice of robbery and murder, and practically led an outlaw life. The

From T. C. Crawford, An American Vendetta . . . (*New York: Belford, Clarke and Company*, 1889), pp. 15–16, 23–25, 70–74.

Hatfields on one side and the McCoys on the other ranged and plundered, and as a necessary consequence their interests often clashed. So the first quarrel began as far back as in 1863, when Harmon McCoy was killed by Ance Hatfield; that is to say, common report credits him with the killing. . . .

In 1882 Ellison Hatfield, with a number of the members of his family, went over on an election day into Pike County, and while there became engaged in a controversy with the McCoys. . . . There had been a dispute about some hogs. Floyd Hatfield had lost some hogs that had strayed among the McCoy pigs, and he had to appeal to a magistrate to recover his property. This most petty of subjects led to a very serious dispute. This dispute was brought to a focus by one of the Hatfields becoming engaged in a quarrel with one of the McCoys over a matter of $1.75, when they began to draw their weapons and show signs of fight. Ellison Hatfield then interfered, and as he did so four of the McCoys closed upon him and killed him. Three of the McCoys stabbed him with their knives. He was cut in at least twenty-four different places.

One of the younger McCoys, who had been represented as being too much of a child to be involved in this murder, was yet the age of sixteen. That is quite old enough for any such affair as this. There are numerous witnesses, moreover, who saw this youngest fellow doing most of the cutting in the back of Ellison Hatfield. Floyd McCoy, who escaped and who never was tried for participation in this murder, is said to have run up and fired a pistol directly against the body of Ellison Hatfield. Elias Hatfield was present, and he came to the rescue of his kinsman, only too late. He chased and ran down one of the leading McCoys, shooting his revolver at him five times in the chase. I had the story of this from Elias Hatfield's own lips. The great Hatfield family, made up of mountaineers, hunters, and strong, daring men, were never so badly hurt in their pride as when Ellison Hatfield fell. They arrested the three McCoys and carried them across the river to the West Virginia side to await the result of the injuries to Ellison Hatfield. Ellison Hatfield was attacked on Monday, and on the following Wednesday he died. After his death a mysterious party took the three McCoys over to the Kentucky side and blew out their brains, leaving them on the ground where they were shot. The Kentucky authorities have indicted the guards who were placed over them for this offense, but Elias Hatfield, who was one of the guards, says that a strong party came up and took possession of the prisoners and went off with them in the darkness and that the guards were in no way responsible.

Common report places the execution—or the murder, just as you please—of these three men upon Ance Hatfield, who is to-day the leader of the Hatfield side. Although Ance Hatfield can probably show that he was not actually present at the killing, yet the credit of it undoubtedly belongs to him.

Ance Hatfield: A Feudist at Home

The scene presented when Ance Hatfield began to discuss the feud was one well worthy of an artist's pencil. The patriarch, at the head of the dominating faction in this great vendetta, himself a tall, powerful man, not showing as yet a single trace of advance in years, sat in an easy pose and talked with recklessness and the grace of an accomplished advocate. At his right, with his chin hanging upon his breast, was Cap Hatfield, the most pronounced type of the human murderer I have ever seen. Back of him sat several guards with their Winchesters across their shoulders. Winchesters gleamed in every direction. They were in rows across the beds, and every now and then the door would open and in would stalk another tall mountaineer. Patrols were continually coming and going. The children swarmed in and out, while the three daughters, clinging together after the fashion of the Three Graces, would move in and out from the darkness of the rear room, or would sit silent in the corner listening with apparent indifference to all that was being said.

The three visitors all wore overcoats, and as we threw back our overcoats it was noticeable that the people we had come to see were nervous. The throwing back of the coat of a stranger has to them a significance that it would not have to the average man. Even John B. Floyd's presence was not sufficient guarantee to produce a perfect feeling of confidence. Ance Hatfield, who discussed many things, and all in a peculiar mountain dialect, was asked by me how it was that in so many of the mountain brawls shots were frequently fired to the number of fifty or sixty, and sometimes two hundred, without any one being hit.

"I will tell you," said he. "The human varmint is the most coorious and most cunningist varmint thar is. When he goes into a fight he turns his body sidewise, so that there is presented for the bullet only four inches of life space, and even that he doesn't hold up fa'r and squar.' He just keeps adodgin' and friskin' about, and so when the bullets come along they don't find him. That is the only way that I can account—for it," said he.

He spoke in a pleasant way of the McCoys, and much regretted the quarrel, but he knew of no way of settling it. People had threatened his life and threatened the lives of his children, and he swore over and over again in every form of emphatic phrase that he would kill those who touched any of his. It was curious to notice the affectionate spirit developed by Ance Hatfield during this conversation, for his children. It might have been a good piece of dramatic acting, but the old gentleman has often enough proved his devotion to his children. He has been out on many a night raid, the purposes of which were simply retaliation and punishment for some insult or injury done his children. He is a man of intense pride. He does not know how to read or write, but he has lived the life of a mountaineer so long that he has imbibed such a spirit of freedom that he will not submit to the dictation of anyone. He is the absolute dictator of the family, and the power of his dominating spirit is well illustrated by Elias Hatfield, who told me that on the night that Jonce Hatfield was arrested he was in Ance Hatfield's house with his wife. When the news came through Rosanna McCoy of the capture of Jonce Hatfield there was a hurried consultation. Ance called on all his followers, and they all turned out but Elias Hatfield. He thought that there might be trouble growing out of the raid, and so he hesitated. His wife, whispering in his ear, pleaded with him to stay at home, but old Ance called out imperiously: "Come with me, or you are no Hatfield"; and so the man of peace, rather than submit to that, turned out to follow the fiery leader, who swept away in the night, and succeeded in accomplishing the object of his mission.

18 / The Pittsburgh Labor Riot of 1877: An Urban Uprising

One of the most violent years in American history was 1877, the year of the great railroad strike that began in Maryland and West Virginia and spread across the country. Wage cuts in a time of depression drove railroad and other workers to the desperate riots that flared first in Baltimore on July 20–21 and then raged out of control in Pittsburgh on July 21–22. The Pittsburgh riot is doubly significant as one of the country's greatest labor upheavals and one of its greatest urban uprisings. The strike and riots of 1877 opened a long era of violent labormanagement conflict, which lasted until the 1930s. Striking similarities

From James D. McCabe [*Edward W. Martin, pseud.*], The History of the Great Riots . . . (*Philadelphia: National Publishing Company, 1877*), *pp. 91–93, 97–103.*

to the great urban riots of the 1960s (Watts, Newark, Detroit) may be noted in the following account. The narrative begins on the night of Saturday, July 21. The riot started earlier in the day when a mob was fired on by militia from Philadelphia.

The mob had now swollen to an enormous size, and was rendered furious by the firing of the Philadelphia troops. By eight o'clock in the evening mobs were moving about the city in various directions, sacking stores to secure arms, breaking into the armories of the military companies, and preparing themselves to execute threats freely expressed of massacring the entire Philadelphia command. The city was at this time virtually in the hands of an utterly irresponsible mob, composed only in small part, however, of railroad hands, but more of laborers and iron workers, coal miners, stevedores, and others who were in full sympathy with the strikers. A large mob visited Johnson's gun factory on Smithfield street, about seven o'clock in the evening and armed themselves. Another still larger crowd demolished Brown's establishment on Wood street, which they completely gutted, and then marched down Fifth avenue, with drums beating and flags flying; about three thousand in number.

The round house and its gallant defenders were now the objects of the fury of the rioters. The soldiers were shut up in this building without food of any kind. By ten o'clock a mob of several thousand people had congregated about the round house, but remained at a respectful distance from it, as it was generally believed that its defenders were prepared to open on the crowd with artillery and Gatling guns in case of an attack. During the night a gun belonging to the Hutchison Battery, that had been left on the hill, was planted by the rioters within one hundred yards of the round house and loaded to the muzzle with couplings and broken rails. A sharp and effective fire was opened by the troops upon the men in charge of this gun, and they were driven off. Repeated efforts were made to discharge the piece, but each man who ventured near it was picked off by the Philadelphians. The next morning thirteen dead bodies, lying near the gun, bore witness to the accuracy of the Philadelphia marksmen. . . .

The firing of the troops in the round house for a moment dismayed the rioters, and they swayed backward. They soon recovered their courage, however, and as thousands were flocking to their assistance, they returned to the attack. Finding it impossible to dislodge the military from the building, they resolved to burn them out. An order to this effect was issued, and it was carried into execution with alacrity. In consequence of the blockade which had existed for two days, the sidings in the yards of the outer station, as well as those extending eastward for three or four miles, were crowded with freight cars, filled with grain produce and merchandise of all kinds, besides which a number of loaded oil, coke, and coal cars were collected there *en masse*. While a portion of the mob surrounded the building in which the military had taken refuge, large bodies proceeded to set fire to the oil cars, and in a moment huge volumes of black smoke rolled upwards, followed by lurid flames reaching out in every direction, telling that the work of the destruction of property had begun.

The sight of the flames seemed to literally craze the rioters, some of whom rushed wildly about with flaming torches in their hands, applying them to the cars indiscriminately. An alarm of fire was sounded and the department promptly responded, but the rioters, who had complete control of the city, refused to permit them to make any effort to extinguish the flames. They said they were determined to destroy the railroad company's property, but would do no injury to that belonging to private citizens. They kept their word, too, and when a lumber pile belonging to a citizen took fire the rioters themselves turned in and helped to extinguish the flames and removed the lumber to a safe place. Train after train was fired by the infuriated crowd, but the cars were so far distant from the round houses that the heat did not seriously affect the military, although their position was one of peril. Finally a large party of strikers captured a car filled with coke, which they ran from the Allegheny Valley Railroad track to a siding connecting with the Pennsylvania Railroad. They then procured large quantities of petroleum oil, and, pouring it over the coke, ignited the materials in a very few moments. The car was soon a mass of fire, and it was then pushed along the tracks and forced against the round house.

The building was soon ignited, and the soldiers were now compelled to prepare to fight their way out through the frenzied mass of humanity clamoring for their blood. The building did not burn as rapidly as was desired, and the mob, bent on revenge, rushed out the road and sent burning trains toward the doomed buildings. From midnight until five o'clock next morning the main efforts of the crowds were directed to firing the buildings and cars, but about half an hour later the mob, which had been besieging the military, left, for some unexplained reason. This afforded the troops, who were in actual danger of being roasted alive, an opportunity to emerge from the building, and they succeeded in reaching Liberty street in a very few moments. They quickly formed in line and marched up to Thirty-third street, and from there to Penn avenue and Butler street. Their objective point was the

United States Arsenal, on Butler street, where they expected to obtain shelter. While turning into Butler street, however, the leaders had discovered their retreat and fully 1,000 men, fully armed and suppiled with ammunition, followed in pursuit. The troops marched at the ordinary pace, and in good order. They were fired upon from the street corners, alley-ways, windows, and housetops, and returned the fire, using once their Gatling guns, and inflicting heavy loss upon their assailants. When they reached the arsenal the commandant refused to admit them. He said he had but ten men, and would be powerless to hold the place if the mob should attack it. He consented to take care of the wounded, and they were accordingly carried into the hospital.

The main body of the troops continued their march out Butler street, a fusilade being kept up on them by the mob as they moved forward. The shots fired killed one of the soldiers. Before they reached the arsenal and nearly opposite the cemetery gate, fully a mile above the arsenal, two others were killed and left lying on the sidewalk. They continued their retreat and crossed over to the north side of the Allegheny river on Sharpsburg bridge, the mob following them as rapidly as possible. After reaching the north side the troops scattered, and in this way the mob was divided into small bodies. The pursuit soon ceased. At Sharpsburg the troops obtained food, after which they resumed their retreat, and after a march of about twelve miles reached a place called Rose's Grove about five o'clock on Sunday afternoon. A brief halt was made there to rest the men, and the division then marched about a mile further, to a hill near Claremont, where the troops bivouacked to await orders.

In the meantime the city was in a state of anarchy. Thousands who had not joined in the pursuit of the retreating troops gathered about the burning buildings and trains, and assisted in spreading the flames wherever they had not been applied. . . .

The scenes transpiring on Liberty street, along the line of which the tracks of the railroad run, simply beggar description. While hundreds were engaged in firing the cars and making certain of the destruction of the valuable buildings at the outer depot, thousands of men, women and children engaged in pillaging the cars. Men armed with heavy sledges would break open the cars, and then the contents would be thrown out and carried off by those bent on profiting by the reign of terror. The street was almost completely blockaded by persons laboring to carry off the plunder they had gathered together. In hundreds of instances wagons were pressed into service to enable the thieves to get away with their goods. Mayor McCarthy early in the day endeavored to stop the pillage, but the handful of men at his command were unable to control the crowd, who were desperate in their anxiety to secure the goods before the pillage was checked, but the mob fired the cars and then proceeded with the work of destruction. It is impossible to form any idea of the amount of goods stolen, but hundreds of thousands will not cover the loss.

Some of the scenes, notwithstanding the terror which seemed to paralyze peaceable, orderly citizens, were ludicrous in the highest degree, and no one seemed to enjoy them with greater zest than those outraged in the wholesale plunder. Here a brawny woman could be seen hurrying away with pairs of white kid slippers under her arms; another, carrying an infant, would be rolling a barrel of flour along the sidewalk, using her feet as the propelling power; then a man pushing a wheelbarrow loaded with white lead; boys hurried through the crowds with large-sized family Bibles as their share of the plunder; while scores of females utilized aprons and dresses to carry flour, eggs, dry goods, etc. Bundles of umbrellas, fancy parasols, hams, bacon, leaf lard, calico, blankets, laces and flour, were mixed together in the arms of robust men or carried on hastily-constructed hand-barrows.

19 / Presidential Assassin: Charles Guiteau, Killer of Garfield, 1881

Of the four assassinated presidents, only one—Lincoln—was the victim of an assassination conspiracy. The other three—Garfield, McKinley, and Kennedy—fell at the hands of lone assassins. Each assassin professed or seemed to act in the interest of a particular ideology: Guiteau (assassin of Garfield) espoused Stalwart Republicanism; Leon Czolgosz (assassin of McKinley) claimed to be an anarchist; and Lee Harvey Oswald (assassin of Kennedy) espoused Marxism. But in each case a closer analysis seems to indicate that mental instability rather than ideology was the root cause of the act.

On July 2, 1881, Charles Guiteau shot President James A. Garfield in the Pennsylvania Railroad station of Washington, D.C. Although Guiteau was found to be sane and ultimately paid with his life for his action, a review of Guiteau's career reveals not the conventional Stalwart Republican and "disappointed office seeker" of the history books but a man who, in retrospect, seems to have been suffering from serious

From John P. Gray, The United States vs. Charles J. Guiteau: Review of the Trial (*reprinted from the* American Journal of Insanity, *January and April, 1882*), pp. 52–54.

mental derangement. The following synopsis of Guiteau's bizarre life was enunciated by the district attorney during Guiteau's trial.

. . . it is shown that this man went from place to place, leaving unpaid board bills behind him; that he borrowed money on false representations, using the names of prominent men as references, without their knowledge or consent, to secure the money; that he abandoned his practice of the profession of law, as he said it did not pay, and went to lecturing on theological subjects, in imitation of prominent evangelists, who, he said, had made money; that while he was professing religion, and a church member, he was guilty of deception and lasciviousness; that in the character of a Christian gentleman, he traveled through the country borrowing money and contracting indebtedness for his personal support, which he seldom if ever paid, though profuse in promises, evasions and misrepresentations; that he published a book called "Truth," a large part of which was stolen from a book published many years before, called the "Berean," that he represented and sold this book "Truth," as his own literary production and ideas; that failing in this he returned to the practice of law, and collected money for clients which he retained; that he associated himself with the Young Men's Christian Association, had his letters addressed in their care, and used his relations with them as a passport to secure confidence, which he grossly abused; that he fraudulently obtained money by burnishing an oroid watch which he passed off for gold, and boasted of it; that he declared that he would secure notoriety by good or evil, even if he had to kill some prominent man and imitate Wilkes Booth; that as far back as 1872, he took part in the Greeley campaign, declaring that he expected by so doing to secure the Chilian mission; that in order to procure a divorce from his wife, who had labored for him, and sent money to him for his support, although he was at the time a lawyer, and as such an officer of the court, yet deliberately, in accordance with his own statement, committed adultery with a prostitute, and appeared as a witness against himself in the divorce proceedings by which a decree of divorce was granted against him.

That during his married life, while a member of the church and professing religion and engaging in the public exercises of the church with which he was connected, got his wife to borrow money of the pastor; and afterwards being accused of immoral conduct and vicious and dishonest practices, and in addition having a loathsome disease, he admitted the truth of the accusation. That he went again into politics, because neither the law nor theology would pay; that he used each and all the schemes he undertook which have been presented as evidences of his insanity for the purpose of dishonestly obtaining money; that during the political campaign of 1880, he wrote a speech which was delivered but once.

That on this speech and his so-called services in the campaign he claimed and asked for an important foreign appointment, and for that purpose came to Washington; that immediately before coming to Washington he was getting a precarious subsistence in New York by soliciting life insurance; that in order to get to Washington, he borrowed ten dollars, and arrived in Washington without funds; that he stopped at the Ebbit House one day, and left without paying his bill; that he went from one boarding house to another in Washington leaving the board bills unpaid in each and falsely representing that he was expecting money and would soon pay; that he borrowed fifteen dollars from a friend, stating that he wanted money to pay a board bill, but really used it to purchase a pistol with which to shoot the President of the United States; that he boarded at a respectable house in the city of Washington for more than five weeks, leaving it only days before the shooting, and only then because the landlady demanded payment for board which he promised to pay in a few days, but which was never paid.

That during this time he was on friendly relations with his fellow-boarders, conversing with them daily at the table upon religious and general topics, attending church, reporting and discussing sermons with the pastor, as well as the revision of the New Testament, and the situation as represented by the Senatorial contest at Albany—and exhibiting nothing unusual in his manners, conduct or conversation; and while stopping at this house he followed the President on at least two occasions, for the purpose of shooting him—once watching him from Lafayette Park, but seeing him ride out with several friends desisted from shooting him; once he followed him to the depot, but seeing his sick wife leaning on his arm refrained from shooting him on that occasion; and during all this time he never mentioned the subject of inspiration, or that he had any extraordinary relation with the Deity, or had any Divine commission to perform; that he went to the Riggs House the day before the shooting, and left that board bill unpaid; that failing to secure the office he sought, and disappointed in the expectations which he had frequently said he confidently entertained, he followed the President from place to place seeking the opportunity to shoot him, and finally learning that the President was to go to Long

Branch on a certain day, he went to the railway station to waylay him, and there stealthily approaching him from behind, treacherously murdered him by shooting him in the back.

That arrested and charged with this crime, he justified it as a patriotic act, and claimed that it was a political necessity, and that the President was guilty of the blackest ingratitude by going back on the men who made him, that in removing the President he took but the life of one man and thereby cemented the Republican party, and prevented another war, which might have cost thousands of lives as our last war did; that he said the prominent men connected with the Republican party, who he supposed would be benefited by his crime, would protect him from the consequences of his act; that when he learned that these men had expressed their abhorrence of his crime, he appeared to be "struck dumb," and in "great mental agony"; and after collecting himself he repeatedly used the words "most astounding," and exclaimed: "What does it mean? I would have staked my life that they would defend me"; and again repeated the words "most astounding"; and that shortly thereafter he, for the first time, used the word or expressed the idea of "inspiration," in referring to his crime; and that only since that time has he claimed inspiration as a defense for the murder.

20 / Anti-Chinese Violence:
The Rock Springs Massacre of 1885

Wherever the Chinese went in the West, prejudice and violence followed them. Basic to anti-Chinese feeling was the white workingman's resentment of the willingness of the Chinese to work long hours for low wages. At times the undercurrent of tension between white and Chinese workers flashed into violence. This happened in Rock Springs, Wyoming Territory, on September 2, 1885. White coal miners in Rock Springs felt that they were being increasingly displaced in the mines by Chinese. A clash on September 2 led quickly to the massacre of some 22 to 50 Chinese and the expulsion of the remaining 400 to 500 others. Public opinion in the West supported the white miners, and in a matter of days the Rock Springs massacre inspired similar but less fatal attacks on Chinese in Idaho, Montana, and Washington. Two accounts follow. The first was "written from notes taken by a gentleman who happened to be pasing through Rock Springs at the time," and the

From Isaac Hill Bromley, The Chinese Massacre at Rock Springs, Wyoming Territory, September 2, 1885 (*Boston: Franklin Press, 1886*), pp. 50–52, 54–55.

second is that of Ah Kuhn, a Chinese, as given in a later hearing on the massacre.

Situated in the south-western part of the Territory, Rock Springs is a place of six hundred or seven hundred inhabitants. The chief industry is coal-mining, and the mines are owned by the Union Pacific Railway Company. For some time the company, through agents, have employed Chinamen in these mines; and on the day of the massacre there were five hundred Celestials [i.e. Chinese] in the Chinese colony, which was located in the east section of the town.

All summer long among the white miners there has been developing a feeling of bitterness against the Chinese, nothing but a pretext being wanted to make an attack. This pretext came Wednesday morning, Sept. 2, when a quarrel arose in the mines, between a white miner and two Chinamen, over the possession of a "room." The fight in the mines became general, and did not end until one Chinaman had been killed, four severely wounded, and several white men badly hurt. All the work in the mines then ceased; the Chinamen going to their settlement, and the white miners returning to town, and arming themselves with any thing that would carry ball or shot. In the mean time, the Chinese had raised a flag of danger in Chinatown, and every Celestial in Rock Springs was making for his quarters. They appeared to realize the danger of their position, and were actively preparing to depart. No sooner had the miners finished their dinners, than they began to assemble in the streets, and "Vengeance on the Chinese!" was the universal cry, even some of the women joining in the demonstration. A vote was then taken, and the immediate expulsion of the Mongolians was determined upon. Seventy-five armed men, followed by a crowd of boys armed with clubs, shovels, picks, and drills, took up their march for Chinatown, proceeding down the railroad-track. There was a party of Chinamen at work beside the railroad, and the shooting opened on them; but they cleared the way in season to escape serious injury. When within a short distance of the settlement, the mob halted, and sent forward a committee to warn the Chinese that they must leave the place within an hour. A reply was received that they would go in that time; but hardly had thirty minutes elapsed before the crowd moved on toward the enemy, yelling like wild men, and shooting every Chinaman who was in sight. The terrible scene that followed cannot be overdrawn. Without making a show of resistance, the Chinese fled towards the mountains, some hatless, some shoeless, and all without their effects. Running after them, firing indiscriminately, came the white miners, now crazed by the reports of the firearms, and groans of the wounded and dying Chinamen who had been shot before they could escape from the settlement, some even before they left their doors.

Fleeing for their lives, the Chinamen shaped their course in the direction of Bitter Creek, the miners in hot pursuit, and shooting as rapidly as the weapons could be loaded. After the Celestials reached the hills, the shooting ceased, and the inhuman mob marched back to Chinatown, and began looting the houses, of which there were about forty—the property of the Union Pacific, and worth probably five hundred dollars each. Every thing of value was taken from the houses, and they were then set on fire. The flames forced out quite a number of Chinamen who had, until then, eluded detection. These poor fellows were either murdered outright, or fatally wounded and thrown into the burning buildings there to be roasted alive. Not less than fifteen met their fate in this way; and there is not but little doubt that there were at least fifty Chinamen killed altogether. All the afternoon and throughout the night, pistol-shots could be heard in the direction of Chinatown. The burning buildings gave the picture a weird coloring, and the first forcible crusade against the Chinese in America will long be remembered by those who participated in or witnessed it.

During the night, guards were placed about the town to protect the property of the citizens, while the expelled Chinamen rested their limbs on the hills several miles distant, but not too far to witness the destruction of their homes. Thursday morning, Chinatown presented a terrible sight. Protruding from the smouldering ruins were the charred remains of eleven Chinamen, and a sickening odor permeated the entire settlement. Clothing, bedding, household utensils, and provisions were scattered about in confusion, and traces of the preceding day's bloody work could be noticed at every turn. To the east of the town, several bodies were recovered of Chinamen who had been shot while endeavoring to escape, and who were left by their companions to suffer and die where they fell. In the morning the Chinamen who sought refuge in the hills came down to the railroad, and Division Superintendent George W. Dickinson ordered them brought to Evanston on a freight-train. The refugees, about four hundred and fifty in number, arrived at Evanston about four o'clock, Thursday afternoon, half starved, and half frightened to death. They were quartered at the Chinese settlement in Evanston, their fellow-countrymen doing every thing possible to provide for their comfort.

Ah Kuhn, an intelligent Chinaman, speaking English after a fashion, and acting accordingly as interpreter and business manager for the Chinese miners, was called, and answered inquiries as follows:—

Gov. Dir. Savage: Where were you on the day this difficulty occurred?

Ans.: I was in No. 3 mine.

Gov. Dir. Savage: When did you first hear that there was any trouble?

Ans.: About half-past nine I hear there was trouble over in No. 6 mine. I go down Rock Springs with China boy to office. I ask for Mr. Evans. I ask him, "You know trouble over in No. 6 mine?" He say yes. He go No. 3 mine; he stop about hour; I wait for him, I want see him again. He drive wagon up to No. 4 mine. I see lots white men (pretty near a hundred) come across from saloon, and go in section-house. White man he knock China boy down with brick on head; boy he holler and come to Chinatown. I stop him, I tell him "Keep still." About a hundred white men go up to No. 3 mine with rifles. All boys get scared and run away. I say, "Come back." Fellow on hill with rifle stop and shot good many times and come down.

Gov. Dir. Savage: Did you see some of the Chinamen shot?

Ans.: No, I down in cellar, no see 'em. I tell Mr. Evans all boys scared. About eight o'clock some boy he come in and take old boxes and pile 'em all together; he say to another boy, "You get some matches?" I feel awful sorry; not know how to get out. He go out about five minutes; I tell him, "Boy better go." Chinese boy he would not go in house; boys hit him; he fall down on the ground, and boys get scared and run. I stay in cellar from three to eight o'clock. About half-past ten I see lots of men coming down from No. 6 mine. Good many have rifles. I go up to No. 3 mine, and tell Mr. Miller he drive wagon over Chinatown. I tell him, "White man make much trouble, driving Chinamen away." Mr. Miller say, "No get scared." Chinamen work in No. 4 room, No. 5 entry; white man come in and drive Chinaman out. Knock China boys down on the ground; boss he send car down and bring China boy out, and send for wagon and take boy back to his camp. About eight o'clock I saw all houses burning up. I come out of cellar. Three or four white men came along and kick door, and say, "You better come out, or we drag you out." I come out, and run about two hundred yards. I turn my head, I look back and see three or four white men standing. He see me, and shot me four times; I fall down and drop the money, and ran up to No. 4 mine. I went down the track across the river. I walk up the track, and see good many China boys, about seventy or eighty. I walk up to the railroad section-house, knock at the door, and say, "Mr., you better open door and let me in." He say, "Who's that?" I say, China boy." He open the door, and let me come into that house. I say, "I am nearly dead, I got nothing to eat." I ask him, "You give me some bread?" He say, "You got some bread." He say, "What's the matter at Rock Springs?" I say, "Lots trouble, drive China boys out." I sat down and took nip of water; took piece of bread and eat 'em; I feel much better; I say, "Mr., you let me have hand-car I go next station." He say, "I have no hand-car." In morning I started back. He say, "You better not go back to Rock Springs," and I went back to Evanston, and came back on the seventh of the month.

21 / The White Caps: A Violent Movement of the Late Nineteenth Century, 1887

Although White Cap violence swept America in the late nineteenth century, today it is almost forgotten. Originating in rural southern Indiana in 1887, the White Cap movement drew upon both the vigilante tradition in regard to extralegal punishment and the Ku Klux Klan tradition in regard to masked violence. In southern Indiana and elsewhere throughout the nation White Cap violence was directed mainly against the immoral, the shiftless, the drunken, and men who abused or failed to support their families. In the South and in the southwest, however, economic discontent was a more significant source of White Cap violence. White Capping lasted well into the twentieth century; while never organized beyond the local level, in time it became a generic term for local violence of various sorts.

"Yes, Sir: the White Caps whipped me last Wednesday," drawled a pale-faced, lazy-looking young man, as he leaned over a rickety fence in the very wildest part of Harrison County, Ind., to answer to a *Times* correspondent's interrogation. The correspondent had heard of several recent outrages and had gone there on his tour of investigation. The name of the individual referred to is Joel Wright, and he lives on a small place in a little hamlet called Shakerville, about eight miles east of Corydon. His property consists of land through which runs a huge ledge of rock. The story of his troubles with the "White Caps" is best told in his own language:

"I am a poor man and live here with my wife and brother-in-law,

From the New York Times, *October 12, 1887, p. 2.*

Ike Allen. I was always sort of weakly and never able to work much, and people said I was lazy, but I tell you the truth, I want to work as much as any one, but I can't; I'm a sick man. Last Wednesday night I was laying here in bed a-sleeping, jist as nice as any one would want to, when something got hold of my throat. I was about half awake by that time and I hollered out: 'My——! Mirandy! (meaning my wife,) Werner's dog has got me.' I saw it was a man, an' I fit till they tied me. Then my wife she screamed an' was bad skeered. The children cried, too, and begged 'em not to hurt me. There were seven of the men, for I counted 'em. One of 'em had a lantern. They was dressed in common clothes, but each had a handkerchief tied across his mouth and nose, an' his hat was pulled down so he could jist see.

"Seein' I couldn't do nothin',' I went with them to a woods near here, where they stripped off my shirt an' tied me to a saplin.' Then one man said: 'Joel, there's been lots of stealin' goin' on 'bout here, and while we don't say you did it, you're a sort of no 'count fellow and don't pervide for yer family. We're goin' to whip you, an' if you don't hump yourself an' go to work we'll come back and give you another beatin'.' This skeered me, but I'm not a nervous man, and I know'd I hadn't done no wrong, so I jist said, kinder pleasant like: 'Gentlemen, if I've done anything wrong I want to hang for it.' "

"That kind of a bluff wouldn't work, though, would it, Joel!" said his wife, who had come out and stood near by, with a smile on her face, while Joel related his experience.

"As I was sayin','" continued Joel, who is a great talker and evidently slightly proud on account of the sudden prominence he has secured by his "White Cap" experience, "one of 'em cut a saplin' and' hit me seven or eight times with it on my bare back. It hurt like blazes, and when I hollered so much they stopped an' run over to their horses, which they got on an' rid away. Joe Brown's boy saw 'em right afterward over there near the cut. My little girl came over an' cut me loose. I ain't over it yet; they hurt me pretty bad."

During the last week no less than 20 men have been taken out in different parts of the county and whipped by white-capped vigilantes. Over in Spencer Township, last week, probably two of the most sensational cases took place. Aaron Bitner, a wealthy farmer over 60 years old, and Squire John Hilderbrand were taken out and whipped until they were nearly dead. They live in a small settlement on Big Indian Creek. At that place the reporter was unable to see the principals, as they were both in bed and their families would not talk about the occurrence. From a talkative neighbor, however, the following particulars were learned:

Bitner was a widower, and about four weeks ago he married a widow with one son about 7 years of age. From the beginning, it is said, Bitner had no affection for the boy and was continually abusing him. The young fellow was pretty wild, and after getting into several scrapes was, it is alleged, unmercifully whipped by his stepfather. A week ago the boy got into trouble again and the story is that Bitner took him out to a shed to punish him. The reporter's informant said that 15 minutes afterward the boy's mother became alarmed and went out to see how the punishment was progressing. To her horror she beheld her son hanging from a rafter with a clothesline around his neck. Near by stood her husband with a fiendish look upon his face. The mother screamed for help, which soon arrived, and after much difficulty the half dead boy was restored to life, but he had a narrow escape, and even now is very ill from the effects of his terrible experience. The story of the alleged brutal outrage was soon noised about, and on Monday about 20 masked men rode into town and, taking Bitner, gave him the whipping he so richly deserved.

Esquire Hilderbrand threatened to kill his wife and daughter, and otherwise behaved very unbecomingly. He was flogged on the same night, and probably earned his punishment, for he was fined and put under bond before Esquire Slaughter on Friday for abusing his family.

Mott Station is just now enjoying a little sensation of almost a similar character. Mott is a very appropriate name for the place, for there are as motley a crowd of people there as one would be able to find anywhere on the face of the globe. On Thursday morning early risers found near the railway station the following expressive note tacked upon a post:

Notice.—Phil Zeiner, Harvey Emily, John Long, and Robert Mott, the whisky ring, had better quit the way they are a-doing. If they don't they will be taken out and whipped. Bob Mott had better leave the county.

WHITE CAPS.

There was great excitement among the men, and Mott immediately sold out and left. . . .

The "White Caps," from what the reporter could learn, are not a gang of lawless ruffians, as one would suppose from reading of their proceedings, but farmers who propose to make the lazier, shiftless population behave themselves. A dollar looks as big to them as a barn door, and in order to save the expense of a court trial they simply consider the case and take the law in their own hands. An instance illustrative of this occurred yesterday, while the reporter was stopping at Gresham station. Bob Morris, a worthless fellow, broke into the railroad station and stole six tickets to Boston. The young lady who has charge traced the theft to him readily, and when she boldly charged him with it he owned up. Twenty minutes afterward a note was left in his front yard, signed by the "White Caps," telling him if he did not leave the place immediately he would be taken out and whipped. No one thought of having him arrested.

22 / A Gay Nineties Mass Murderer: H. H. Holmes, 1890–94

In recent years Americans have been shocked by a succession of mass murders (e.g., in 1966 Charles Whitman with 13 victims in Austin, Texas, and Richard Speck with 8 victims in Chicago), but the mass murderer is nothing new in our history. Perhaps the most prolific of all mass murderers was H. H. Holmes (alias of Herman Webster Mudgett), who confessed to having killed 27 persons from about 1890 to 1894. Many of the victims met their fate in a weird castle-like building that Holmes operated as a rooming house for visitors to the Chicago world's fair of 1893. Although Holmes later repudiated his confession, it seems to have been largely true. Found guilty of the murder of Benjamin F. Pitezel, Holmes was hanged on May 7, 1895.

After alluding to a repeated desire for a detailed confession, and a tribute to Detective Geyer for his marvelous work in unearthing his villanies, Holmes stated that his first victim was Dr. Robert Leacock, of New Baltimore, Mich., whom he killed by a dose of laudanum in order to secure a large sum of insurance money. Being now in full possession of a thirst for murder, and with a conscience conveniently stifled, Holmes stated that his second victim was Dr. Russell, a tenant of his in the Chicago house, now known as the "Castle." This time the murder was done by a blow from a heavy chair, and Holmes' next care was to make a safe disposition of the body. This he accomplished by selling it to a dealer in such merchandises, thus establishing a

From Frank P. Geyer, The Holmes-Pitezel Case . . . (*Philadelphia: n.p., 1896*), pp. 504–08.

business connection profitable to both parties interested. This dealer Holmes stated paid him a sum ranging from $25 to $45 for each body, and resold them as dissecting material. Mrs. Julia L. Connor was claimed by Holmes to have been the third person to meet death at his hands, and an alleged criminal operation was given as a partial cause of her death. The death by poison of her little daughter, Pearl Connor, was the fourth in Holmes' list, and he shifted a portion of the responsibility of this crime on to a man and a woman, whose names he withheld.

West Morgantown, Va., furnished Holmes the fifth person whose murder he added to his roll of crimes. Rodgers was the name, and it was upon a fishing trip that Holmes ended this man's life by a blow upon the head with an oar. This body was found after about a month had elapsed.

A southern speculator by the name of Charles Cole, visited Chicago after some correspondence with Holmes, who eventually enticed the southerner to "The Castle." He was destined to become number six on the list, being despatched by a confederate while Holmes engaged him in conversation. The weapon employed this time was a piece of gas pipe, and the blow was so vicious that it impaired the market value of the body when offered to the usual person for disposal. The janitor of "The Castle" was named Quinlan, and Holmes claimed that he paid too much attention to a domestic named Lizzie. He decided that Lizzie would better die before the intimacy progressed so far that he would have to part with Quinlan. So Lizzie furnished the seventh victim, and a certain peculiarly constructed vault in "The Castle" was the scene of her death. Holmes claimed that her murder was the first committed in this death chamber, and that, before suffocating her, she was compelled to write letters to relatives informing them that she had left Chicago for some point further west. According to Holmes, the numbers eight, nine and ten in this fatal lottery, were drawn by a Mrs. Sarah Cook, her unborn child and a Miss Mary Haracamp of Hamilton, Canada. His story was that Mrs. Cook with her husband and niece kept house in "The Castle," and that he boarded with them. The fact that these women had access to all parts of the house, and that they suddenly came upon him while preparing his last victim for shipment made it necessary to despatch both quickly. With his accustomed celerity in such matters, he had the pair into the fatal vault and took their lives after compelling them to write a letter to Mr. Cook, stating that being tired of living with him, they had left the city and would not return. Holmes alluded to their deaths as being "particularly sad," as both women were "exceptionally upright and virtuous."

Pursuing his story of horrors, Holmes next told the story of the death of Miss Emmeline Cigrand, of Dwight, Illinois—the eleventh person to meet death at his hands. He told how she was employed by him as a stenographer—and became almost indispensable to him in that capacity, and had become his mistress as well. That she was on the point of being married to a young man whose life he had vainly tried to take, and of his resolve to murder her, accomplishing this by luring her to the fatal vault, where she met death in a slow and lingering form. An unsuccessful attempt to murder three young women who worked in Holmes' restaurant on Milwaukee street, Chicago, was next dwelt upon, as was the fact that he would have received $90 for the three bodies if he had been able to deliver them. Holmes attributed his failure in this instance to his foolish attempt to chloroform all of them at once. It seemed that they escaped from him and ran into the street. He stated that he was arrested the next day, but was not prosecuted for what he had done. Then followed a statement that as he had attempted to murder Mrs. Pitezel and two of her children, failing through no fault of his own—these unsuccessful attempts at murder might justly be added to the number he had accomplished. Holmes stated in regard to his next victim—who was a beautiful young woman by the name of Rosine Van Jassand—that he used more caution than formerly, and compelled her to live with him in his fruit and confectionery store for some time before poisoning her with ferro-cyanide of potassium. He claimed to have buried her body in the basement of the store, as it would have been dangerous to remove a large box from this place. This murder counts for number twelve.

Suggestions for, perhaps, the most horrible of the murders Holmes related, were those furnished by his account of Robert Latimer, who was in his employ. He stated that this man had more or less knowledge of his guilty secrets, and had endeavored to obtain money as the price of his silence. The secret room and slow starvation were his fate instead, followed by the usual transaction between his murderer and the purveyor for medical colleges. He told of Latimer's attempt upon the solid walls of his prison with his unaided hands, and how something of an excavation was found by the police when the horrors of "The Castle" were exposed. Latimer was number thirteen, according to Holmes.

Holmes then went on to tell how he procured the death of Miss Anna Betts, by the substitution of a poisonous ingredient in a prescription she had filled at his drug store in "The Castle." This was his fourteenth murder, and the next one described by him, that of Miss Gertrude Connor, of Muscatine, Iowa, was brought about in the same way, although this lady reached her home in Iowa before she died. This murder was not the next in the sequence of crime, but was given in connection with that of Miss Betts, on account of the similarity of the circumstances. Holmes claimed to have acted as agent for a young woman of Omaha, whose name in full he did not give, and to have induced her to go to Chicago to take advantage of a favorable opportunity for converting her real estate into cash. This Miss Kate ───── after the necessary papers were signed, was lured into the fatal vault and never came out again alive. This was murder number sixteen.

In the description of his next capital crime, Holmes told how, under the supervision of a Mr. Warner, of the Warner Glass Bending Co., a large kiln of fire-brick was built in the basement of "The Castle" for the purpose of exhibiting his patents. It was so constructed that iron could be melted in less than one minute by means of crude oil and steam. Inducing the inventor to go inside, Holmes stepped out and turned on both oil and steam. There was no body for sale this time, as not even the bones of his victim remained. Number eighteen. Holmes and a young Englishman who was associated with him in business, enticed to Chicago a banker from a North Wisconsin town. Holmes said that once within the secret room they forced him to sign drafts for seventy thousand dollars by means of depriving him of food and nauseating him with gas; also that by his partner's skill at forgery these were converted into money, and that his confederate killed the man with chloroform, while he disposed of the body in the usual way.

Holmes claimed to have forgotten the name of his nineteenth victim, but remembered that she boarded at "The Castle" restaurant, and later lived in the building with a man who eventually assisted him in murdering her. This time Holmes administered the chloroform while his tenant prevented her struggles. The twentieth and twenty-first numbers in the calendar of crime stood for the Williams sisters. Holmes told, at considerable length, of his acquaintance with them, of his defrauding them of their money, of Nannie Williams' murder in the vault, and how he poisoned Minnie Williams near Momence, Ill. Again Holmes' memory failed him for the name of a man whom he used in some business capacity, but he remembered killing him and burying the body in the basement of a house near the corner of Seventy-fourth and Honore streets, in Chicago. Another murder, of which he remembered all the particulars, was that of Baldwin Williams, whom he said he shot in Leadville, Colorado, under circumstances that made it appear that the shooting was done in self-defence. So far the roll of Holmes' victims footed up to twenty-three, and to them he added those with which the reader is already familiar, Benjamin F. Pitezel, Howard, Alice, and Nellie Pitezel, in the order named.

23 / The Lynching of Eleven Italians: New Orleans, March 14, 1891

In 1890 New Orleans police chief David Hennessy was fatally shot in an ambush. Two Italian factions had been carrying on a feud for the control of banana loading on the New Orleans waterfront. Chief Hennessy was considered to be hostile to one of them, the Matrangas —supposedly a Mafia faction. Members of the Matranga faction were tried for Hennessy's murder and acquitted on March 13, 1891. The next day a mob headed by leading citizens stormed the jail and killed 11 Matranga factionists who had been charged with the Hennessy murder. The application of lynch-law in one of the oldest and most important cities of the nation as late as 1891 was a shocking illustration of the persistence of extralegal violence in American history. The brutal episode involved a convergence of the vigilante tradition, the Southern lynch-law tradition, and prejudice against Italians. The mass lynching brought the United States to the brink of war with Italy and spurred a wave of anti-Italian feeling throughout the country.

In every paper in the city this morning appeared the following call:

"All good citizens are invited to attend a mass meeting on Saturday, March 14, at 10 o'clock A. M., at Clay Statue, to take steps to remedy the failure of justice in the Hennessy case. Come prepared for action." . . .

The verdict of the jury in the Hennessy case had startled and angered everybody. The statements of the jury bore out the suspicion that the members had been purchased. Consequently at 10 o'clock there was a large crowd at Clay Statue on Canal Street. . . . There was a crowd of young and old men, black and white, but mostly of the best element. Speeches were made by Messrs. Parkerson, Denegre, and Wickliffe. . . .

[After Parkerson and Denegre spoke to the crowd] Mr. J. C. Wickliffe followed in the same denunciatory manner, saying among other

From the New York Times, *March 15, 1891, p. 1.*

things that self-preservation is the first law of nature, and that the time had now come for the citizens of New-Orleans to protect themselves.

> If such action as the acquittal of these assassins is to be further tolerated, if nothing is done to forcibly portray the disapproval of the public of this infamous verdict, not one man can expect to carry his life safe in the face of organized assassination that so powerfully exists in our midst as to openly set law and order at defiance. We met in Lafayette Square to talk. We now meet at the foot of Henry Clay's statue to act. Let us therefore act, fellow-citizens. Fall in under the leadership of W. S. Parkerson. James D. Houston will be your First Lieutenant, and I, J. C. Wickliffe, will be your Second Lieutenant.

Arms had been provided at Royal and Bienville for about fifty men, and the members of the committee who had called the assemblage went there, secured pistols and shotguns, and then the crowd marched on the Parish Prison.

The starting of the crowd had an electric effect on the city. Soon the streets were alive with people running from all directions and joining the main body, which moved sullenly down Rampart Street to the jail near Congo Square. Doors and windows were thrown open, and men, women, and children crowded on the galleries to encourage those who were taking part and to witness the scene.

When the main crowd from Canal Street reached the prison a dense throng had already collected there, all eager to take a hand in whatever might happen. When the vanguard of armed citizens reached the jail, which is many squares from Canal Street, that grim old building was surrounded on all sides. . . .

Meanwhile, the prisoners were stricken with terror, for they could hear distinctly the shouts of people without, madly demanding their blood. Innocent and guilty alike were frightened out of their senses, and those who were charged with crimes other than complicity in the murder of the Chief also shared in the general demoralization. Some of the braver among the representatives of the Mafia wanted to die fighting for their lives, and they pleaded for weapons with which to defend themselves, and when they could not find these they sought hiding places. The deputies, thinking to deceive the crowd by a ruse, transferred the nineteen men to the female department, and there the miserable Sicilians trembled in terror until the moment when the doors would yield to the angry throng on the outside.

Capt. Davis refused the request to open the prison, and the crowd began the work of battering in the doors. Around on Orleans Street there was a heavy wooden door, which had been closely barred in anticipation of the coming of the avenging mass. This the crowd selected as their best chance of getting in. Neighboring houses readily supplied axes and battering rams and willing hands went to work to force an opening. This did not prove a difficult task to the determined throng. Soon there was a crash, the door gave way, and in an instant armed citizens were pouring through the small opening, while a mighty shout went up from 10,000 throats. There was more resistance for the intruders, however, but it too was soon overcome with the huge billet of wood which a stout man carried. Then the turnkey was overpowered and the keys were taken from him.

By that time the excitement was intense, none the less so when a patrol wagon drove up with a detachment of policemen, who were driven away under a fire of mud and stones. When the leaders inside the prison got possession of the keys the inside gate was promptly unlocked, and the deputies in the lobby promptly got out of harm's way. The avengers pressed into the yard of the white prisoners. The door of the first cell was open and a group of trembling prisoners stood inside. They were not the men who were wanted, and the crowd very quickly, though with remarkable coolness, burst into the yard. Peering through the bars of the condemned cell was a terror-stricken face which some one mistook for Scoffedo. A volley was fired at the man and he dropped, but none of the shots struck him, and it was subsequently found that he was not one of the assassins. The inmates of the jail were ready to direct the way to where the Italians were.

"Go to the female department," some one yelled, and thither the men, with their Winchesters, ran. But the door was locked. In a moment the key was produced. Then the leader called for some one who knew the right men, and a volunteer responded and the door was thrown open. The gallery was deserted, but an old woman, speaking as fast as she could, said the men were upstairs. A party of seven or eight quickly ascended the staircase, and as they reached the landing the assassins fled down at the other end. Half a dozen followed them. Scarcely a word was spoken. It was the time for action. When the pursued and their pursuers reached the stone court yard the former darted toward the Orleans side of the gallery and crouched down beside the cells. Being unarmed they were absolutely defenseless. In fear and trembling they screamed for mercy. But the avengers were merciless, and a deadly rain of bullets poured into the crouching figures.

Gerachi, the closest man, was struck in the back of the head, and his body pitched forward and lay immovable on the stone pavement.

Romero fell to his knees, with his face in his hands, and in that position was shot to death.

Monastero and James Caruso fell together under the fire of half a dozen guns, the leaden pellets entering their bodies and heads, and the blood gushing from the wounds.

The executioners did their work well, and beneath the continuing fire Cometex and Trahinia, two of the men who had not been tried, but who were charged jointly with the other accused fell together. Their bodies were literally riddled with buckshot, and they were dead almost before the fusillade was over.

When the group of assassins was discovered on the gallery, Macheca, Scoffedi, and old man Marchesi separated from the other six and ran upstairs. Thither half a dozen men followed them, and as the terror-stricken assassins ran into cells they were slain. Jo Macheca, who was charged with being the arch-conspirator, was a short, fat man, and was summarily dealt with. He had his back turned when a shot struck him immediately behind the ear, and his death was instantaneous. There was no blood from the wound, and when the body was found the ear was swollen so as to hide the wound, which the Coroner had great difficulty in locating.

Scoffedi, one of the most villainous of the assassins, dropped like a log when a bullet hit him in the eye. Old man Marchesi was the only one who was not killed outright. He was struck in the top of the head while he stood beside Macheca, and though he was mortally wounded, he lingered all the evening before dying.

Pollize, the crazy man, was locked up in a cell upstairs. The doors were flung open and one of the avengers, taking aim, shot him through the body. He was not killed outright and in order to satisfy the people on the outside, who were crazy to know what was going on within, he was dragged down the stairs and through the doorway by which the crowd had entered. A rope was provided and tied around his neck and the people pulled him up to the crossbars. Not satisfied that he was dead, a score of men took aim and poured a volley of shot into him, and for several hours the body was left dangling in the air.

Bagnetto was caught in the first rush upstairs and the first volley of bullets pierced his brain. He was pulled out by a number of stalwart men through the main entrance to the prison and from the limb of a tree his body was suspended, although life was already gone.

Just as soon as the bloody work was done Mr. Parkerson addressed the crowd, and asked them to disperse. This they consented to do with a ringing shout, but first they made a rush for Parkerson, and lifting him bodily, supported him on their shoulders while they marched up the street. The avengers came back in a body to the Clay statue and then departed. Immense crowds rushed from all directions to the neighborhood of the tragedy, while the streets in front of the newspaper offices were blocked with people anxious to see the latest bulletins.

W. S. Parkerson, who was the Captain of the mob, was the political leader of the Democracy of 1888, and is one of the leading lawyers of the city. James D. Houston, who was announced as First Lieutenant, is also a prominent political leader. John C. Wickliffe, the Second Lieutenant, is one of the editors of the *New Delta*. He is a Kentuckian and a West Pointer. The mob's work was done quickly and without unnecessary violence. No one was injured but the men against whom there was proof of complicity in the assassination of the late Chief of Police, and men who are known to be active agents of the Mafia. The shotguns and ropes of the mob have executed eleven men. Public sentiment condemned the men indicted for the crime; public action has put them to death. The city is unanimous in upholding the action of the mob.

24 / Racism and Sadism: The Lynch-Burning of a Black Man in 1899

Following the era of Reconstruction the lynching of blacks in the Southern and border states was practiced to terrorize them and to maintain white supremacy. From 1882 to 1927 as many as 3,405 blacks were lynched in 17 Southern and border states. Folk tradition held that blacks were lynched only for the crimes of rape or murder, but the statistics reveal that they were also frequently killed for lesser offenses or for no other reason than prejudice. The lynchings became increasingly brutal and sadistic. Burning of the hapless victim became quite common and was accompanied, often, by unspeakable mutilation and torture. Typical was the fate of Richard Coleman, who was tortured and burned to death in Maysville, Kentucky, on December 6, 1899, for the murder of his white employer's wife. From the jail in Covington, Kentucky, the authorities had taken Coleman back to Maysville, where the lynching occurred.

Richard Coleman, colored, the confessed murderer of Mrs. James

From the New York Times, *December 7, 1899, p. 1.*

Lashbrook, wife of his employer, expiated his crime in daylight to-day by burning at the stake after suffering torture and fright beyond description, at the hands of a mob of thousands of citizens.

The dreadful spectacle occurred on the peaceful Cricket Grounds on the outskirts of this, one of the oldest and among the proudest cities of Kentucky. The barbarities inflicted upon this young negro are almost beyond belief, and can only be accounted for by the intense horror created by long consideration of the atrocious crime of which full confession had been made by Coleman. . . .

. . . Coleman had been told . . . to prepare to return to the scene of his crime. He was stricken with fear, and begged piteously to be permitted to remain in Covington until after his trial. He said he expected to die, but he dreaded the vengeance of a mob. When he was handcuffed on leaving the jail in Covington he was almost paralyzed, and had to be assisted to the patrol wagon. The crowd about the jail there and at the Covington station added to his fear. On entering the train he seemed unable to sit down, until one of the guards forced him into a seat. It developed that in the crowd at Covington, and even on the train, there were some of the relatives of Mrs. Lashbrook, ready to convey information if any attempt was made to secrete the prisoner. . . .

The prisoner with his escort arrived [at Maysville] at 10:20 [A.M.] o'clock. . . . As the train pulled slowly into the old station the mob formed on both sides. Armed men stationed themselves at the platforms of all the cars and warned the frightened passengers to remain quiet and not to interfere. . . .

At the Court House a mob of over 2,000 men, headed by James Lashbrook, the husband, had been hastily formed. A demand for the prisoner was made, accompanied by threats from the leaders. There was a brief struggle in which weapons were hastily drawn by the officers, and then the Sheriff and his assistants were overcome by force of numbers, and the prisoner was pulled from among them. Up through the centre portion of the town the mob marched, the prisoner being held by the vanguard and dragged along with the aid of ropes loosely attached to his body. He was the target of hundreds of missiles, and several times he sank half conscious to the ground while the crowd pressed forward, striking at him with clubs, sticks, and whips until his head and body were scarcely recognizable. More dead than alive, he was dragged along and forced to his feet. Scores of women joined the men. High above the noise, the wretch could be heard pleading for his life. This spectacle continued until the grounds were reached where the final work of the mob, was accomplished. . . .

The place of execution had been selected weeks ago, in accordance with all the other arranged details of the programme mapped out by the leaders of the mob. The prisoner was dragged to the sapling and strapped against the tree, facing the husband of the victim. Large quantities of dry brush and larger bits of wood were piled around him while he was praying for speedy death. James Lashbrook, the husband of the victim, applied the first match to the brushwood. A brother of the victim struck the second match. Some one with a knife was slashing at the prisoner's chest. By a sort of cruel concurrence of action on the part of the mob not a single shot was fired. The purpose seemed to be to give the wretch the greatest possible amount and duration of torture. As the flames arose Coleman's horror increased and he made vain efforts to withdraw his limbs from the encroaching fire. The ropes securing him to the tree were burned and his body finally fell forward on the burning pile. Even then, although it was not certain whether he was living or dead, the vengeful purpose of the crowd led them to use rails and long poles to push his body back into the flames. It is not certain how long life lasted. . . .

During the process, while his voice could be heard, he begged for a drink of water. At the end of three hours the body was practically cremated. During all that time members of the family of Mrs. Lashbrook had remained to keep up the fire and keep the body in a position where it would continue to burn. It is said that on the march through the city the prisoner's eyes had been burned out by acid thrown in an eggshell. In all the thousands who constituted the mob there was not a single effort made to disguise or conceal identity. No man wore a mask. All the leaders of the mob are well known and there are hundreds of witnesses who can testify to their participation in the tragedy. They are leading citizens in all lines of business and many are members of churches. . . .

The coroner held an inquest on the charred remains of Richard Coleman and rendered the simple verdict, "Death at the hands of a mob." The body was left lying there. Relic hunters took away teeth and bones and flesh and every fragment of the body that they could lay hands on. All the afternoon children, some of them not more than six years old, kept up the fire around the blackened body by throwing grass, brush, bits of boards, and everything combustible that they could get together. This they kept up until dark. . . .

IV

VIOLENCE IN
THE TWENTIETH CENTURY

25 / Presidential Assassin: Leon Czolgosz,
Killer of McKinley, 1901

On September 6, 1901, Leon Czolgosz, a self-styled anarchist, fatally shot President William McKinley in Buffalo, New York, where the latter had gone to attend the Pan-American Exposition. Czolgosz was subsequently convicted of the crime and executed. The following selections indicate that Czolgosz had been shy and withdrawn as a child and adolescent and mentally unstable as an adult. Although he claimed to have shot McKinley in the interest of the anarchist movement, the organized anarchists (whom Czolgosz had contacted) were disconcerted by his strange manner, suspected him of being a spy for the authorities, and rejected him. The selections are from Walter Channing, a prominent psychiatrist of the day. The final selection consists of his conclusions about Czolgosz.

Czolgosz as Child and Adolescent

As a little child the father says Leon was quiet and retired. It was hard for him to get acquainted with other children; he cared to play with only a few. If he was angry he would not say anything but he had the appearance of thinking more than most children. He sometimes did not want to do what he was told, but perhaps not more so than other children. . . . As he grew older he was very bashful. . . . The father does not remember that he had any chum or intimate acquaintance of either sex and never saw him in company with any girl.

From Walter Channing, "The Mental Status of Czolgosz, the Assassin of President McKinley," American Journal of Insanity, XLIX (1902–3), 238, 254–55, 278.

Examination by Medical Experts
in Buffalo Following the Crime

On the part of the government this was made by Drs. Fowler, Crego and Putnam. The following is an extract from their examination:

His height is 5 feet 7⅝ths inches, age 28, weight when in Buffalo 136 pounds. General appearance that of a person in good health. Complexion fair. Pulse and temperature normal. Tongue clean, skin moist and in excellent condition. Pupils normal and react to light, reflexes normal, never had any serious illness. He had a common school education, reads and writes well. Does not drink to excess, although drinks beer about every day, uses tobacco moderately, eats well, bowels regular. Shape of his head normal as shown by the diagram obtained by General Bull, Superintendent of Police with a hatter's impress.

In the first interview on Sept. 7th, he said:

I don't believe in the Republican form of government, and I don't believe we should have any rulers. It is right to kill them. I had that idea when I shot the President, and that is why I was there. I planned killing the President 3 or 4 days ago after I came to Buffalo. Something I read in the *Free Society* suggested the idea. I thought it would be a good thing for the country to kill the President. When I got to the grounds I waited for the President to go into the Temple. I did not see him go in but some one told me he had gone in. My gun was in my right pocket with a handkerchief over it. I put my hand in my pocket after I got in the door; took out the gun, and wrapped the handkerchief over my hand. I carried it in that way in the row until I got to the President; no one saw me do it. I did not shake hands with him. When I shot him I fully intended to kill him. I shot twice. I don't know if I would have shot again. I did not want to shoot him at the Falls; it was my plan from the beginning to shoot him at the Temple. I read in the paper that he would have a public reception. I know other men who believe what I do, that it would be a good thing to kill the President and to have no rulers. I have heard that at the meetings in public halls. I heard quite a lot of people talk like that. Emma Goldman was the last one I heard. She said she did not believe in government or in rulers. She said a good deal more. I don't remember all she said. My family does not believe as I do. I paid $4.50 for my gun. After I shot twice they knocked me down and trampled on me. Somebody hit me in the face. I said to the officer that brought me down, "I done my duty." I don't believe in voting; it is against my principles. I am an anarchist. I don't believe in marriage. I believe in free love. I fully understood what I was doing when I shot the Presi-

dent. I realized that I was sacrificing my life. I am willing to take the
consequences. I have always been a good worker. I worked in a wire
mill and could always do as much work as the next man. I saved three
or four hundred dollars in five or six years. I know what will happen
to me,—if the President dies I will be hung. I want to say to be published—"I killed President McKinley because I done my duty. I don't
believe in one man having so much service, and another man should
have none."

At the Sept. 8th interview he said he had heard Emma Goldman
lecture, and had also heard lectures on free love by an exponent of
that doctrine. He had left the church 5 years ago because as he said,
he "didn't like their style." He had attended a meeting of the anarchists about six weeks ago and also in July. Had met a man in Chicago
about ten days ago who was an anarchist and talked with him.

The Friday before the commission of this crime he had spent in
Cleveland, leaving Buffalo, where he had been for two or three weeks,
and going to Cleveland. "Just went there to look around and buy a
paper." The circle he belonged to had no name. They called themselves Anarchists. . . . During this examination the prisoner was very
indignant because his clothing was soiled at the time of arrest, and he
had not had an opportunity to care for his clothing and person as he
wished. . . . He said he would have slept well last night but for the
noise of people walking about. He heard several drunken people
brought into the station at night. Said he felt no remorse for the crime
he had committed. Said he supposed he would be punished, but every
man had a chance on trial; that perhaps he wouldn't be so badly
punished after all. His pulse on this occasion was 72—temperature
normal; not nervous or excited.

Channing's Evaluation of Czolgosz' Mental State

It will be apparent from a careful perusal of what has already been
said what conclusions I think I am justified in arriving at:

1st. I feel that from fuller information than that possessed by those
experts who examined Czolgosz after his crime, the opinion then expressed by them cannot be accepted as the final one.

2d. Owing to lack of time it was impossible in the examination referred to, to investigate the early history of Czolgosz. Had this been
done some of his statements would have been found to be inaccurate.

3d. He was not in my opinion an anarchist in the true sense of the
word, and while anarchist doctrines may have inflamed his mind and

been a factor in the crime, it was not the true cause or an adequate explanation.

4th. He had been in ill health for several years, changing from an industrious and apparently fairly normal young man into a sickly, unhealthy and abnormal one.

5th. While in this physical and mental condition of sickness and abnormality, it is probable that he conceived the idea of performing some great act for the benefit of the common and working people.

6th. This finally developed into a true delusion that it was his duty to kill the President, because he was an enemy of the people, and resulted in the assassination.

7th. His conduct after the crime was not inconsistent with insanity.

8th. His history for some years before the deed; the way in which it was committed and his actions afterward furnish a good illustration of the typical regicide or magnicide. . . .

9th. The post-mortem examination threw no light on his mental condition and would not invalidate the opinion that the existing delusion was the result of disturbed brain action.

10th. Finally, from a study of all the facts that have come to my attention, insanity appears to me the most reasonable and logical explanation of the crime.

26 / Harry Orchard: Labor Union Dynamiter and Assassin, 1904–5

The conflict between management and labor unions in the western United States was especially violent. Much of the violence took place in the mining industry, where mine owners and unionists were equally tough and determined. Spearheading the union drive was the Western Federation of Miners (W.F.M.) under its relentless dynamic leader, William (Big Bill) Haywood. The mine owners responded with brutal suppressive tactics, and the W.F.M. fought back—literally for its life. The union did not hesitate to resort to dynamiting and assassination. Its most effective hired killer was Harry Orchard (alias of Albert E. Horsley), an experienced practitioner of the explosive art. In the selections below Orchard describes two of his most famous exploits: the blowing up of the Independence, Colorado, railroad depot platform on

Albert E. Horsley (alias Harry Orchard), The Confessions and Autobiography of Harry Orchard (*New York: The McClure Company, 1907*), pp. 129, 135–36, 197–98, 217–18.

June 6, 1904, and the assassination of former Idaho governor Frank Steunenberg in Caldwell, Idaho, on December 30, 1905. The bombing of the Independence depot took place in the course of the bitter labor war of 1903–04 in the Cripple Creek mining district. Steunenberg had gained the ill will of the W.F.M. by anti-union actions while serving as governor of Idaho.

Blowing Up the Independence Depot, 1904

During the wrangle Pettibone, Davis, and Parker said I had better go to Cripple Creek and blow up something. . . . I told them it would not be much trouble to blow up the Independence depot. We had talked about this before. The idea was to get the night shifts of non-union miners that got on the 2:30 train there every morning. They said that would be all right. . . .

About eleven o'clock, when 'most everybody around there had gone to bed, we [Orchard and Steve Adams] took the two fifty-pound boxes of powder with us and went over to the depot. This depot had been closed for some time, and they kept no operator there, though the train stopped there for people to get on and off. The depot was built on a side-hill, with a long platform in front of it. We walked under this platform, and I crawled under where the plank came right close to the ground. I dug away a little place in there, and buried the two boxes of dynamite in the ground close up to the planks, put in the giant-caps and set up the windlass on one of the boxes, and filled the two little bottles with sulphuric acid from another bottle I had it in. This was ticklish business as it was very dark in there, and I had to fill these little bottles without seeing them; and though I kept a pasteboard over the giant-caps and the dynamite while I was filling this, yet a drop of acid would have set the whole thing off. We had a mixture of sugar and potash on the caps, too, that the acid would set fire to immediately.

Then we stretched a wire out from the windlass about two hundred feet on to a spur track, and tied a chair-rung to the end of it. We went back to an old ore house beside the spur track and waited. It had been dark and lowery that night, but about two o'clock it began to lighten up. We were a good deal put out by this, as there was a small moon and it got quite light. The train we were waiting for came in every evening about 2:30, and it generally was on the dot. We heard the men come on the platform talking, and finally we heard the train. Then we got down to the end of the wire and took hold of the chair-rung, and when the train was within about a hundred feet of the depot, we each had a hold of one end of this chair-rung which the wire was attached to, and pulled it and kept right on going. We intended to take the wire with us, but forgot that part, as the rocks and débris were falling around us pretty thick, although neither of us got hurt. I do not know how many men were on the platform at the time, but I think there were thirteen killed outright and some others maimed and crippled for life.

We ran as fast as we could, and soon got up on the railroad and followed it around nearly to the old Victor mine on the north side of Bull Hill, and then separated.

The Assassination of Frank Steunenberg, 1905

. . . Haywood said he wanted to get ex-Governor Steunenberg before he left the office, and further said he had sent two or three men down there to get him, but they had all failed. . . .

Moyer said he thought it would have a good effect if we could bump Steunenberg off and then write letters to Peabody, Sherman Bell, and some others that had been prominent in trying to crush the Federation, and tell them that they, too, would get what Governor Steunenberg got; that we had not forgotten them, and never would forget them, and the only way they would escape would be to die. . . .

I was playing cards in the saloon at the Saratoga, and came out in the hotel lobby at just dusk, and Mr. Steunenberg was sitting there talking. I went over to the post-office and came right back, and he was still there. I went up to my room and took this bomb out of my grip and wrapped it up in a newspaper and put it under my arm and went down-stairs, and Mr. Steunenberg was still there. I hurried as fast as I could up to his residence, and laid this bomb close up to the gate post, and tied a cord into a screw-eye in the cork and around a picket of the gate, so when the gate was opened, it would jerk the cork out of the bottle and let the acid run out of the bottle and set off the bomb. This was set in such a way, that if he did not open the gate wide enough to pull it out, he would strike the cord with his feet, as he went to pass in. I pulled some snow over the bomb after laying the paper over it, and hurried back as fast as I could.

I met Mr. Steunenberg about two and a half blocks from his residence. I then ran as fast as I could, to get back to the hotel if possible before he got to the gate. I was about a block and a half from the hotel when the explosion of the bomb occurred, and I hurried to the hotel as fast as I could.

27 / The Kentucky Night Riders and the Hopkinsville Raid, 1907

In 1904 Kentucky and Tennessee tobacco farmers organized in a peaceful cooperative, the Planters' Protective Association, in order to obtain higher prices for their crops. Since 1890 the American Tobacco Company and other domestic and foreign buyers had used their control of the market to drive down the prices that the growers received for their produce. It was against this state of affairs that the farmers organized. But the tactics of nonviolence did not succeed, and in 1906 the planters turned to violence through the illicit Night Rider movement. Farmers who did not join the cooperative were beaten and had their tobacco plant beds destroyed. Soon the Night Riders took to raiding towns and destroying the warehouses of the large tobacco companies. Twenty-five of these raids occurred. The most sensational was the raid—executed with military precision—of December 6, 1907, on Hopkinsville, one of the largest towns of western Kentucky. The Night Rider movement was broken up in 1908 by the authorities, but the farmers did gain their objective of higher tobacco prices.

Shortly before 2 o'clock this morning two hundred night riders, most of whom were masked and all heavily armed, invaded Hopkinsville and in an hour of untold horror, with the red glare in the sky of three great burning buildings, houses of good citizens were riddled with bullets, many acts of wantonness and brutality were performed and anarchy reigned. . . .

After completing their work the night riders quietly departed from town. They were pursued ten or twelve miles by a posse of eleven men under Deputy Sheriff Lucien H. Cravens, and near Gracey a pitched battle occurred in which the posse believes at least one night rider was shot.

The night riders marched into town via the Illinois Central tracks. They had left their horses at the crossing of the Cadiz road and the railroad, about two miles from the city. Reaching the Illinois Central station they proceeded to break the glass in six windows with butts of guns, but not finding Operator McDavid in the office they circled the building and started at a brisk gait up Ninth street.

A squad of about twenty men besieged police headquarters and

From the Louisville Courier-Journal, *December 8, 1907, pp. 1, 3–4.*

wrecked the doors and windows by firing scores of shots. Policemen Broderick, Claxton and Miller were kept under guard during the invasion. Misses Annie Curtis and Lillian Boyd were on duty at the Cumberland telephone office. The street door and the inside door of the building were locked, but the marauders smashed out the glass and eight of them went upstairs into the operators' room and made the young women leave their instruments and go with them down on the street. Miss Maud Brown was the only operator on duty at the Home company's office, she being on the second floor, and no attempt was made to reach her.

Before the night riders reached the main portion of town the alarm had been given by some one on the west side, and Miss Brown at once rang in the fire alarm, but so quickly had the invaders moved that before the fire department could get out the invaders had surrounded the central fire station and with leveled guns kept the firemen back in the station, threatening to shoot both men and horses if an attempt was made to bring out the wagons.

Earnest Hayden, one of the firemen, stuck his head out of a window and immediately one of the masked men shot at him, but the bullet did not strike him. From there to the L. and N. station was only a short distance, and here they captured Night Operator Will Owen and took him to Ninth and Liberty streets, where he was held under guard with several other citizens who had been captured. Prior to capturing the operator the night riders shot out three windows in the waiting room.

The independent warehouse of M. H. Tandy & Co. was then fired, entrance being gained by breaking in the front door. Coal oil was used liberally and almost in an instant the entire building, which covered an entire square, was a mass of flames, and from the fire here the warehouse adjoining, occupied by R. M. Woolridge & Co. as a storage house for the Planters' Protective Association, was set on fire, and this also was completely destroyed. . . .

Seeing that the Tandy warehouse was beyond saving the night riders marched in military array up Campbell street to the warehouse of Tandy & Fairleigh representing the Italian Regie contractors. Ed Shanklin, the watchman at this place, heard the footsteps of the men as they marched up the street and, securing his gun, he went down into the basement of the building. He escaped from the burning building after the raiders left it. The night riders broke into the office, first pouring in a volley of shot from weapons of every description, duplicated their free use of coal oil, and this building, which belonged to W. T. Tandy, also was a total ruin.

They then marched up to Seventeenth street and back to Main and Ninth streets, where they mobilized and counted off numbers instead of names and marched out the Illinois Central tracks, as they had come.

So sudden had been the invasion and so well-planned were their operations and so successful were the carrying out of these plans, only one person fired at the night riders while they were in the city, although the mob fired hundreds and hundreds of shots in volleys, and at times there was a perfect hail of bullets on the housetops.

While the mob was at police headquarters Joe McCarroll, Jr., stepped from his house and fired ten times at them with a repeating rifle. Blood on the pavement indicates that someone was wounded. They returned the fire and McCarroll retreated to the house. . . .

The property loss will amount to fully $200,000, with from $40,000 to $50,000 insurance. On the warehouse belonging to John C. Latham no insurance was carried with local agents. On the warehouse owned by W. T. Cooper the loss is covered, as was the building occupied by Tandy & Fairleigh. The tobacco in all the buildings was insured. Tandy & Fairleigh and M. H. Tandy & Co. will make no statement on their losses. The Regie concern is said to have had about 100,000 pounds of tobacco, and the floor had about 25,000 pounds, worth from eight to ten cents a pound.

The association warehouse had twenty-eight hogsheads worth about $150 a hogshead.

Lindsay Mitchell, the buyer for the imperial company, was brutally mistreated. He and Mrs. Mitchell had been up all night with their ill child at their boarding-house on South Main street. The raiders surrounded the place and began firing into it. They shouted for Mr. Mitchell to come out to them. Mrs. Mitchell went to the door and pleaded with the men to leave, telling them of the sickness of her baby. When Mrs. Mitchell appeared on the threshold the muzzles of many guns were thrust in her face and she was harshly bidden to send her husband out. The men, with oaths, shouted to Mr. Mitchell that unless he appeared they would blow up the house with dynamite. They promised not to injure him in any way. Mr. Mitchell having slipped on his clothes, walked out among the men. One of them said: "Mitchell, we are not going to hurt you—" Before he completed the sentence another night man cried, "Yes, —— ——, we are," and struck him on the head with the butt of a gun. With that several of the mob began a brutal assault on the tobacco man and cut gashes on his head and face until he was bleeding in a dozen places. They carried him to the intersection of Main and Ninth streets and kept

him there while the other night men were collecting to leave.
With five men as a guard, Mr. Mitchell was sent back to his home.
The raiders gleefully pointed out to him the burning buildings and
gloated over the ease with which they had accomplished their purpose.

As the invaders were marching up Campbell street, the Rev. George
H. Means, pastor of the Methodist church, appeared at the window
of his bedroom. The men halted and began firing at him. Thirty-two
bullet holes were counted in his room to-day, but he was not injured.
Mrs. Charles Stowe, in the same neighborhood, was fired upon in the
same manner and one bullet struck within an inch of her head. Eight
bullets were fired into Judge W. P. Winfrey's residence on Virginia
street at his son James.

Senator Frank Rives, on the same street, was ordered back into his
room when he looked out of a window.

The damage to plate and windows alone is estimated at from $1,500
to $3,000. A majority of the business houses on Main and Ninth streets
show marks of the fusillades and scores of residences were shot up.
The front of the Kentuckian office, of which Mayor Charles M.
Meacham is editor, was wrecked. The big plate-glass windows on the
ground floor were smashed into smithereens, this seemingly being
done by butts of guns or some other implement. The ground and
stained glass just above these windows show a few holes, while the
windows on the second floor were shot out. Six or eight bullet holes
are also in the east window. The City Judge's office probably shows
more bullet holes than does any other one place in town. As near as
they could be counted there were 177 bullets which passed through
this window. One side window in the entrance to this building was
ruined. The police office was riddled with heavy shot, these in some
instances passing through the room. The wooden front door was filled
full of lead, the bullets, all of which were from shotguns, and were
mostly buckshot, passing through the light wood and burying in the
walls.

Some shot went through the front window and the back door,
being directly in line, the bullets passed entirely through this. Both the
Home and the Cumberland Telephone Companies suffer heavily. The
poles along Ninth and Campbell streets were in many instances burned
off or down entirely. The wires were burned or broken, and the
heaviest loss comes in the melting and destruction of the heavy cables.
It will be days before the telephones in that section are repaired and
in working order.

Many citizens were taken in charge in a manner similar to the following experience:

William E. Graves, who resides on South Virginia street, heard the shots and went out to investigate. He was taken in charge at Twelfth street by five men, who covered him with guns and marched him to Ninth street. As they passed Golay & Hurt's livery stable the men saw a negro named Will Carpenter standing at a telephone near a window in the office.

"Take your head in, —— —— ——," the men yelled, and began firing. Bullets whizzed by the negro's head and his escape from death was remarkable. The window was shattered. Mr. Graves, after this incident, was taken on to Ninth street, where a number of other citizens were being guarded. After being kept there while the raiders made ready to withdraw from the city, and Mr. Graves was compelled to accompany them to the Illinois Central bridge, where they turned him loose and he returned to town.

Lieutenant of Police Booth Morris had been at his home on Fourteenth street only a few minutes when he heard the first firing that announced the arrival of the mob. He hurried down town and ran into three raiders, who covered him with guns and took his revolver from him. They marched him down to the bank of the river and kept him there until the marauders were ready for their ride to Trigg.

It was only a few minutes after the departure of the mob that eleven citizens who had been kept in their houses as prisoners by the complete system of patrolling the streets, armed themselves and, as a sheriff's posse, started in pursuit on horseback and vehicles.

The posse first came in sight of the night riders at the crossing of the Illinois Central railroad and the Cadiz road, where the marauders were mounting their horses for the return trip. Hearing the approaching of the posse, the night riders put whip and spur to their horses and went down the road at full speed, the posse hard behind. From that point to a mile the other side of Gracey, or well inside the confines of Trigg county, the pursuit was kept up, the posse at times coming near enough to exchange shots with the fleeing band.

A pitched battle was fought finally, which continued several minutes. Maj. E. B. Bassett, who was with the posse, had a hand-to-hand conflict with several raiders, who were in a carriage. He had leaped into the vehicle, pistol in hand, and ordered them to surrender. The horse, under the whip of the driver, plunged forward. Maj. Bassett fell under the wheels and the men escaped.

Having no jurisdiction in Trigg county, the posse abandoned the chase. They brought back to Hopkinsville as mementos of their hard ride a bloody handkerchief and a man's hat. The finding of the handkerchief gives ground for the belief that in the running fight between the posse and the nightriders that at least one bullet took effect. It is possible that the hat which was recovered will prove valuable evidence in the future. The last seen of the nightriders they were continuing their way into Trigg county.

28 / Oppressive Management:
The Ludlow Massacre, 1914

In the endemic labor violence that scarred America after the great strikes and riots of 1877 no event—not even the Haymarket Square riot in 1886 or the Homestead strike of 1892—exceeded in violence, bitterness, and tragedy the battle at Ludlow, Colorado, on April 20, 1914, between militia and strikers. The Ludlow massacre was the climactic episode in Colorado's "Thirty Years' War"—a sporadic conflict of strikes and violence between mine owners and workingmen that began in the early 1880s. The Ludlow confrontation stemmed from the strike of the United Mine Workers against Colorado Fuel & Iron (owned by the Rockefeller family) and the other coal mining companies of southern Colorado. The strike—called mainly to gain union recognition—began in September 1913. The strikers at Ludlow and other towns left their company-owned dwellings and moved into their own "tent cities." Later the state militia was sent into the coal region to preserve order and protect mine property. The stage was set for the events of April 20 that shocked the nation: the gun battle between militia and strikers, the burning of the Ludlow tent city, and the death by suffocation of 13 women and children in the "Black Hole of Ludlow." One key element in the violence was the ethnic hostility of the militia to the strikers, who were largely of Greek, Spanish-American, and other "foreign" extraction.

The Ludlow Tent Colony and the Battle

Containing approximately 1,000 people, the Ludlow colony was the largest and most strategically located union camp. . . .

The Ludlow colony was under the command of Louis Tikas, an

George S. McGovern, The Colorado Coal Strike, 1913–14 (*Unpublished Ph.D. Dissertation, Northwestern University, 1953*), pp. 275–76, 279–82, 285–89, 291–95. Published by permission of George S. McGovern.

intelligent Greek strike leader who was praised by all parties to the strike, including militia officers, for his restraining influence upon his Greek compatriots. . . . He was loved and admired by men, women, and children alike at the Ludlow colony because of his deep concern for their welfare and his keen understanding of strike problems. . . .

Although there were some twenty-two nationalities represented in the miners' tent city, the Greeks, largely young unmarried men, were regarded by militia officers as the dominant group. They were determined to prosecute the strike in a vigorous manner and reacted strongly to the bullying tactics of guardsmen such as Linderfelt. . . .

Apparently the residents of the tent colony had become alarmed as they saw the militia maneuvering in the area. It cannot definitely be determined, but they may have learned either, by observation or by wire tapping, of [Major] Hamrock's order to bring the machine gun to Water Tank Hill. Three women from the colony reportedly added the final ingredient to the tension by excitedly reporting the presence of the troops on Water Tank Hill. This report sent an estimated group of from thirty-five to fifty armed Greeks into the sand cut near the colony while other armed men fled with their families in the opposite direction to the protective walls of the arroyo in back of the colony, an arroyo spanned by a heavy steel bridge which offered additional protection. Tikas apparently realized the futility of trying to stop the fleeing men and, according to the military officers, was seen running from the tent village carrying his rifle and field glasses.

Although there are eyewitnesses and participants on both sides who still bitterly insist that one side or the other started the twelve hour battle of April 20, most of the exact details of the initial firing and of subsequent events were lost in the hysteria, noise, and confusion of the day. The explanation offered by the Ludlow military commission seems to be the most reasonable one and was accepted by most of the more competent investigators. According to this account, Major Hamrock, after talking with General Chase in Denver, ordered the explosion of two crude bombs to warn the troops in the area of an expected battle. As nearly as it can be determined these explosions were the first of the day, although some witnesses asserted that rifle fire began before the bombs were exploded. In any case, the explosions were immediately interpreted by the union people as an attack upon one of their positions, at which point they apparently opened fire on the troops. It was not surprising that both sides were convinced that the other was guilty of precipitating the gunfire.

Thus began the desperate battle that was to rage all day, followed by hours of fire, pillage, and horror. . . . Throughout the day the strikers fired from the railroad embankment southeast of the colony, from the arroyo north of the colony, and from the colony itself—supposedly from rifle pits. The troops were armed with Springfield rifles and at least two machine guns and were supported after the battle got under way by mine guards, other mine employees, and the unorganized members of Troop A who were not yet in uniform. An estimated 177 men opposed the strikers after the battle got well under way. Most of the militia firing came from Water Tank Hill where two machine guns were in action, from a row of steel railroad cars standing on the tracks near the colony, and from houses, stores, and other buildings near the mines entrenched north of the colony. . . .

The number of fatalities at Ludlow may never be known for certain. Five strikers and one boy were killed by gunfire, while one soldier was fatally shot early in the battle. . . .

. . . after a day of hard fighting, the militia had driven the strikers from the arroyo and steel bridge north of the colony and readied themselves for a charge on the tent village itself. The tide of the battle was perhaps turned in favor of the militia by the arrival at dusk of reinforcements sent out by the Trinidad sheriff.

The Burning of the Tent Colony

As the charging troops reached the colony, "there rose up," said Linderfelt, "the most awful wail I ever heard in my life."

The screams of terrified women and children drowned out the war cry of the soldiers and according to the militia was the first indication that many of the union families had remained in the colony throughout the day. Some of the soldiers exerted considerable effort to rescue the families, but their efforts were hampered by the terror of the women and children who believed that the troops were taking them out of their dugouts to kill them. Also the board floors which covered the pits, in some instances, made it difficult to conduct a hurried search.

The rescue action of a few of the officers was countered by the brutal behavior of many militiamen, who became an uncontrollable, murderous, pillaging mob when they reached the colony. These soldiers deliberately applied torches to the tents which had not yet caught fire. They looted and smashed their way through the miners' homes, systematically destroying what they were unable to steal. In the words of the investigating militia officers themselves, the militia "had ceased to be an army and had become a mob." The officers frankly admitted that the troops were determined to wipe out every vestige of the union tent village.

The Killing of Louis Tikas

. . . in spite of the pleas of his men, Tikas returned to the tent colony where he was captured by the troops sometime later as he attempted to assist a woman and two children escape from one of the cellars.

Linderfelt, who had previously threatened to "get" the union leader now had his opportunity. Surrounded by his men, the burly lieutenant greeted his captive, "Oh, it's you, God-damned lousy red neck." Then as Tikas replied, the lieutenant seized his army rifle by the barrel and brought it crashing down on the head of the defenseless prisoner with such force that the stock of the heavy gun was broken. Muttering that he had ruined a good rifle, Linderfelt turned and walked away not looking back as three rifle bullets tore into Tikas' back. It could not be determined whether Tikas died from the crushing blow on the head or from the bullets that struck him a moment later. Linderfelt's explanation for the blow was that Tikas had called him "a name that no man will take." He explained the outrageous shooting by his men that followed with the remark, "the damned son-of-a-bitch. He tried to escape."

The "Black Hole of Ludlow"

On Tuesday morning, April 21, the sun shone on what might well be considered the most pathetic scene in the history of industrial warfare. The Ludlow colony which had for seven months been the scene of laughter and heartache, violence and love, was now a miserable shambles. Here and there an iron bedstead, a stove, a child's toy, bits of broken pottery and glass marked the former site of a tent. The charred floors were strewn with the personal belongings of the colorful European nationalities that had comprised the colony. Militiamen stalked through the wreckage surveying the devastating results of their work of the night before, the dark holes under the tents now exposed to their gaze. Then came the discovery which horrified the entire nation and which threw the strikers into a frenzy of grief and uncontrollable rage. Huddled together in one of the larger pits were the lifeless bodies of two young mothers and eleven small children. . . .

The thirteen innocent victims found in "the Black Hole of Ludlow" included Mrs. Patricia Valdez, 37, and her four children: Elvira, 3 months; Eulala, 8, Mary, 7, and Rudolph, 9; Mrs. Cedilano Costa, 27, and her children: Onofrio, 6, and Lucy, 4; and the five children of Mrs.

Alcarita Pedregone and Mrs. Mary Petrucci, both of whom survived the ordeal: Gloria Pedregone, 4, Roderlo [Pedregone], 6, Frank Petrucci, 6 months, Lucy, 3, and Joe, 4.

The underground room in which the women and children died measured eight and one-half by four and one-half feet, its air space probably too small, under conditions of smoke and fire, to maintain an adequate oxygen supply for the women and children who sought refuge there. . . . What probably killed the occupants was the heavy smoke from the burning tent which poured into the opening to the cave, coupled with the depletion of oxygen in the flames above the hole. Mrs. Pedregone saw a soldier set fire to the tent colony and then, half dazed and terror-stricken, she and Mrs. Petrucci, the other survivor, watched their children and the other occupants suffocate. Still apparently stunned by the event, Mrs. Petrucci, months later, described the night of horror. Her tent was in the corner of the colony where the fire started; she believed it was the first tent set ablaze. While the militia shot at her, she fled with her three infants to the pit in a nearby tent. As she sought refuge in the dugout she discovered that it was already occupied by three women and their eight children. An estimated ten minutes later, the tent was on fire. Believing that they were safe from the bullets and the flames, the women seemed to overlook the danger of suffocation. In a comparatively short time they were all unconscious. Early the next morning Mrs. Petrucci and Mrs. Pedregone revived sufficiently to climb out of the hole. After hours of aimless wandering in a dazed condition, they were finally informed that their children were all dead.

The news of the pitiful scene at Ludlow and the casualties among their own ranks was too much for the strikers to bear. Joined by outraged laboring men and sympathizers . . . they struck back furiously against the wanton killing of union families. Colorado became the scene of an open rebellion of hundreds of armed men who held the coal counties under a reign of terror and violence for days. [The violence ended when federal troops were called in to restore peace.]

29 / The Twentieth-Century Race Riot, Communal Type: Chicago, 1919

Until the 1960s the typical American race riot of the twentieth century was the communal *or* contested area *riot involving "a direct struggle between the residents of white and Negro areas." This is in contrast to the predominant* commodity *riots of the 1960s which are character-ized by a black "outburst against property and retail establishments, plus looting." (For a discussion of the commodity riot, see selection 32 of this volume.) The general nature of the communal race riot is elaborated below by sociologist Morris Janowitz. Among the greatest of the communal riots was the Chicago race riot of 1919. It is described and analyzed below by the Chicago Commission on Race Relations.*

Morris Janowitz on the Communal Race Riot

During World War I and its aftermath, the modern form of the race riot developed in Northern and border cities where the Negro was attempting to alter his position of subordination. These outbreaks had two predisposing elements. First, relatively large numbers of new migrants—both Negro and white—were living in segregated enclaves in urban centers under conditions in which older patterns of accommodation were not effective. The riots were linked to a phase in the growth and transformation of American cities. Second, the police and law enforcement agencies had a limited capacity for dealing with the outbreak of mass violence and often conspired with the white rioters against the Negro population. The historical record indicates that they did not anticipate such happenings.

The riots of this period could be called "communal" riots or "contested area" riots. They involved ecological warfare, because they were a direct struggle between the residents of white and Negro areas. The precipitating incidents would come after a period of increasing tension and minor but persistent outbursts of violence. For example, the Chicago riot of 1919 was preceded by 2 years of residential violence in which more than 27 Negro dwellings were bombed. Typically, the precipitating incident would be a small-scale struggle between white and Negro civilians—often in a public place such as a beach or in an area of unclear racial domain. In the major riots of the large cities, tension and violence would spread quickly throughout various parts of the larger community. Thus, deaths and injuries were the result of direct confrontation and fighting between whites and Negroes.

Within a few hours the riot was in full swing, and continued inter-

From *Morris Janowitz, "Patterns of Collective Racial Violence," in Hugh Davis Graham and Ted Robert Gurr, eds.,* Violence in America: Historical and Comparative Perspectives: A Report to the National Commission on the Causes and Prevention of Violence, 2 vols. (*Washington: Government Printing Office, 1969*), II, 319–20.

mittently with decreasing intensity for a number of days. Whites invaded Negro areas and very often the riot spread to the central business district where the white population outnumbered the Negroes. Much of the violence took place on main thoroughfares and transfer points as Negroes sought to return to their homes or sought some sort of refuge. Symbolically, the riot was an expression of elements of the white community's impulse to "kick the Negro back into his place."

The Chicago Race Riot, July 27–August 2, 1919

Thirty-eight persons killed, 537 injured, and about 1,000 rendered homeless and destitute was the casualty list of the race riot which broke out in Chicago on July 27, 1919, and swept uncontrolled through parts of the city for four days. By August 2 it had yielded to the forces of law and order, and on August 8 the state militia withdrew.

A clash between whites and Negroes on the shore of Lake Michigan at Twenty-ninth Street, which involved much stone-throwing and resulted in the drowning of a Negro boy, was the beginning of the riot. A policeman's refusal to arrest a white man accused by Negroes of stoning the Negro boy was an important factor in starting mob action. Within two hours the riot was in full sway, had scored its second fatality, and was spreading throughout the south and southwest parts of the city. Before the end came it reached out to a section of the West Side and even invaded the "Loop," the heart of Chicago's downtown business district. Of the thirty-eight killed, fifteen were whites and twenty-three Negroes; of 537 injured, 178 were whites, 342 were Negroes, and the race of seventeen was not recorded.

In contrast with many other outbreaks of violence over racial friction the Chicago riot was not preceded by excitement over reports of attacks on women or of any other crimes alleged to have been committed by Negroes. It is interesting to note that not one of the thirty-eight deaths was of a woman or girl, and that only ten of the 537 persons injured were women or girls. In further contrast with other outbreaks of racial violence, the Chicago riot was marked by no hangings or burnings.

The rioting was characterized by much activity on the part of gangs of hoodlums, and the clashes developed from sudden and spontaneous assaults into organized raids against life and property.

In handling the emergency and restoring order, the police were

From *The Chicago Commission on Race Relations*, The Negro in Chicago: A Study of Race Relations and a Race Riot (*Chicago: University of Chicago Press*, 1922), pp. 1–7, 601–2.

effectively reinforced by the state militia. Help was also rendered by deputy sheriffs, and by ex-soldiers who volunteered.

In nine of the thirty-eight cases of death, indictments for murder were voted by the grand jury, and in the ensuing trials there were four convictions. In fifteen other cases the coroner's jury recommended that unknown members of mobs be apprehended, but none of these was ever found. . . .

Background of the Riot

The Chicago riot was not the only serious outbreak of interracial violence in the year following the war. The same summer witnessed the riot in Washington, about a week earlier; the riot in Omaha, about a month later; and then the week of armed conflict in a rural district of Arkansas due to exploitation of Negro cotton producers.

Nor was the Chicago riot the first violent manifestation of race antagonism in Illinois. In 1908 Springfield had been the scene of an outbreak that brought shame to the community which boasted of having been Lincoln's home. In 1917 East St. Louis was torn by a bitter and destructive riot which raged for nearly a week, and was the subject of a Congressional investigation that disclosed appalling underlying conditions.

This Commission, while making a thorough study of the Chicago riot, has reviewed briefly, for comparative purposes, the essential facts of the Springfield and East St. Louis riots, and of minor clashes in Chicago occurring both before and after the riot of 1919.

Chicago was one of the northern cities most largely affected by the migration of Negroes from the South during [World War I]. The Negro population increased from 44,103 in 1910 to 109,594 in 1920, an increase of 148 per cent. Most of this increase came in the years 1916–19. It was principally caused by the widening of industrial opportunities due to the entrance of northern workers into the army and to the demand for war workers at much higher wages than Negroes had been able to earn in the South. An added factor was the feeling, which spread like a contagion through the South, that the great opportunity had come to escape from what they felt to be a land of discrimination and subserviency to places where they could expect fair treatment and equal rights. Chicago became to the southern Negro the "top of the world."

. . . Friction in industry was less than might have been expected. There had been a few strikes which had given the Negro the name of "strike breaker." But the demand for labor was such that there were plenty of jobs to absorb all the white and Negro workers available. This condition continued even after the end of the war and demobilization.

In housing, however, there was a different story. Practically no new building had been done in the city during the war, and it was a physical impossibility for a doubled Negro population to live in the space occupied in 1915. Negroes spread out of what had been known as the "Black Belt" into neighborhoods near-by which had been exclusively white. This movement . . . developed friction, so much so that in the "invaded" neighborhoods bombs were thrown at the houses of Negroes who had moved in, and of real estate men, white and Negro, who sold or rented property to the newcomers. From July 1, 1917, to July 27, 1919, the day the riot began, twenty-four such bombs had been thrown. The police had been entirely unsuccessful in finding those guilty, and were accused of making little effort to do so.

A third phase of the situation was the increased political strength gained by Mayor Thompson's faction in the Republican party. Negro politicians affiliated with this faction had been able to sway to its support a large proportion of the voters in the ward most largely inhabited by Negroes. Negro aldermen elected from this ward were prominent in the activities of this faction. The part played by the Negro vote in the hard-fought partisan struggle is indicated by the fact that in the Republican primary election on February 25, 1919, Mayor Thompson received in this ward, 12,143 votes, while his two opponents, Olson and Merriam, received only 1,492 and 319 respectively. Mayor Thompson was re-elected on April 1, 1919, by a plurality of 21,622 in a total vote in the city of 698,920; his vote in this ward was 15,569, to his nearest opponent's 3,323, and was therefore large enough to control the election. The bitterness of this factional struggle aroused resentment against the race that had so conspicuously allied itself with the Thompson side.

As part of the background of the Chicago riot, the activities of gangs of hoodlums should be cited. There had been friction for years, especially along the western boundary of the area in which the Negroes mainly live, and attacks upon Negroes by gangs of young toughs had been particularly frequent in the spring just preceding the riot. They reached a climax on the night of June 21, 1919, five weeks before the riot, when two Negroes were murdered. Each was alone at the time and was the victim of unprovoked and particularly brutal attack. Molestation of Negroes by hoodlums had been prevalent in the vicinity of parks and playgrounds and at bathing-beaches.

On two occasions shortly before the riot the forewarnings of serious racial trouble had been so pronounced that the chief of police sent several hundred extra policemen into the territory where trouble seemed imminent. But serious violence did not break out until Sunday afternoon, July 27, when the clash on the lake shore at Twenty-ninth Street resulted in the drowning of a Negro boy.

The Beginning of the Riot

Events followed so fast in the train of the drowning that this tragedy may be considered as marking the beginning of the riot.

It was four o'clock Sunday afternoon, July 27, when Eugene Williams, seventeen-year-old Negro boy, was swimming offshore at the foot of Twenty-ninth Street. This beach was not one of those publicly maintained and supervised for bathing, but it was much used. Although it flanks an area thickly inhabited by Negroes, it was used by both races, access being had by crossing the railway tracks which skirt the lake shore. The part near Twenty-seventh Street had by tacit understanding come to be considered as reserved for Negroes, while the whites used the part near Twenty-ninth Street. Walking is not easy along the shore, and each race had kept pretty much to its own part, observing, moreover, an imaginary boundary extending into the water.

Williams, who had entered the water at the part used by Negroes, swam and drifted south into the part used by the whites. Immediately before his appearance there, white men, women, and children had been bathing in the vicinity and were on the beach in considerable numbers. Four Negroes walked through the group and into the water. White men summarily ordered them off. The Negroes left, and the white people resumed their sport. But it was not long before the Negroes were back, coming from the north with others of their race. Then began a series of attacks and retreats, counter-attacks, and stone-throwing. Women and children who could not escape hid behind débris and rocks. The stone-throwing continued, first one side gaining the advantage, then the other.

Williams, who had remained in the water during the fracas, found a railroad tie and clung to it, stones meanwhile frequently striking the water near him. A white boy of about the same age swam toward him. As the white boy neared, Williams let go of the tie, took a few strokes, and went down. The coroner's jury rendered a verdict that he had drowned because fear of stone-throwing kept him from shore. His body showed no stone bruises, but rumor had it that he had actually been hit by one of the stones and drowned as a result.

On shore guilt was immediately placed upon a certain white man by several Negro witnesses who demanded that he be arrested by a white policeman who was on the spot. No arrest was made.

The tragedy was sensed by the battling crowd and, awed by it, they gathered on the beach. For an hour both whites and Negroes dived for the boy without results. Awe gave way to excited whispers. "They" said he was stoned to death. The report circulated through the crowd that the police officer had refused to arrest the murderer. The Negroes in the crowd began to mass dangerously. At this crucial point the accused policeman arrested a Negro on a white man's complaint. Negroes mobbed the white officer, and the riot was under way.

One version of the quarrel which resulted in the drowning of Williams was given by the state's attorney, who declared that it arose among white and Negro gamblers over a craps game on the shore, "virtually under the protection of the police officer on the beat." Eye witnesses to the stone-throwing clash appearing before the coroner's jury saw no gambling, but said it might have been going on, but if so, was not visible from the water's edge. The crowd undoubtedly included, as the grand jury declared, "hoodlums, gamblers, and thugs," but it also included law-abiding citizens, white and Negro.

This charge, that the first riot clash started among gamblers who were under the protection of the police officer, and also the charge that the policeman refused to arrest the stone-thrower were vigorously denied by the police. The policeman's star was taken from him, but after a hearing before the Civil Service Commission it was returned, thus officially vindicating him.

The two facts, the drowning and the refusal to arrest, or widely circulated reports of such refusal, must be considered together as marking the inception of the riot. Testimony of a captain of police shows that first reports from the lake after the drowning indicated that the situation was calming down. White men had shown a not altogether hostile feeling for the Negroes by assisting in diving for the body of the boy. Furthermore a clash started on this isolated spot could not be augmented by outsiders rushing in. There was every possibility that the clash, without the further stimulus of reports of the policeman's conduct, would have quieted down.

Chronological Story of the Riot

After the drowning of Williams, it was two hours before any further fatalities occurred. Reports of the drowning and of the alleged conduct of the policeman spread out into the neighborhood. The Negro crowd from the beach gathered at the foot of Twenty-ninth Street. As it became more and more excited, a group of officers was called by the policeman who had been at the beach. James Crawford, a Negro, fired into the group of officers and was himself shot and killed by a Negro policeman who had been sent to help restore order.

During the remainder of the afternoon of July 27, many distorted rumors circulated swiftly throughout the South Side. The Negro crowd from Twenty-ninth Street got into action, and white men who came in contact with it were beaten. In all, four white men were beaten, five were stabbed, and one was shot. As the rumors spread, new crowds gathered, mobs sprang into activity spontaneously, and gangs began to take part in the lawlessness.

Farther to the west, as darkness came on, white gangsters became active. Negroes in white districts suffered severely at their hands. From 9:00 P.M. until 3:00 A.M. twenty-seven Negroes were beaten, seven were stabbed, and four were shot.

Few clashes occurred on Monday morning. People of both races went to work as usual and even continued to work side by side, as customary, without signs of violence. But as the afternoon wore on, white men and boys living between the Stock Yards and the "Black Belt" sought malicious amusement in directing mob violence against Negro workers returning home.

Street-car routes, especially transfer points, were thronged with white people of all ages. Trolleys were pulled from wires and the cars brought under the control of mob leaders. Negro passengers were dragged to the street, beaten, and kicked. The police were apparently powerless to cope with these numerous assaults. Four Negro men and one white assailant were killed, and thirty Negro men were severely beaten in the street-car clashes.

The "Black Belt" contributed its share of violence to the record of Monday afternoon and night. Rumors of white depredations and killings were current among the Negroes and led to acts of retaliation. An aged Italian peddler, one Lazzeroni, was set upon by young Negro boys and stabbed to death. Eugene Temple, white laundryman, was stabbed to death and robbed by three Negroes.

A Negro mob made a demonstration outside Provident Hospital, an institution conducted by Negroes, because two injured whites who had been shooting right and left from a hurrying automobile on State Street were taken there. Other mobs stabbed six white men, shot five others, severely beat nine more, and killed two in addition to those named above.

Rumor had it that a white occupant of the Angelus apartment house had shot a Negro boy from a fourth-story window. Negroes besieged the building. The white tenants sought police protection, and about 100 policemen, including some mounted men, responded. The mob of about 1,500 Negroes demanded the "culprit," but the police failed to find him after a search of the building. A flying brick hit a policeman. There was a quick massing of the police, and a volley was fired into the Negro mob. Four Negroes were killed and many were injured. It is believed that had the Negroes not lost faith in the white police force it is hardly likely that the Angelus riot would have occurred.

At this point, Monday night, both whites and Negroes showed signs of panic. Each race grouped by itself. Small mobs began systematically in various neighborhoods to terrorize and kill. Gangs in the white districts grew bolder, finally taking the offensive in raids through territory "invaded" by Negro home seekers. Boys between sixteen and twenty-two banded together to enjoy the excitement of the chase.

Automobile raids were added to the rioting Monday night. Cars from which rifle and revolver shots were fired were driven at great speed through sections inhabited by Negroes. Negroes defended themselves by "sniping" and volley-firing from ambush and barricade. So great was the fear of these raiding parties that the Negroes distrusted all motor vehicles and frequently opened fire on them without waiting to learn the intent of the occupants. This type of warfare was kept up spasmodically all Tuesday and was resumed with vigor Tuesday night.

At midnight, Monday, street-car clashes ended by reason of a general strike on the surface and elevated lines. The street-railway tie-up was complete for the remainder of the week. But on Tuesday morning this was a new source of terror for those who tried to walk to their places of employment. Men were killed en route to their work through hostile territory. Idle men congregated on the streets, and gang-rioting increased. A white gang of soldiers and sailors in uniform, augmented by civilians, raided the "Loop," or downtown section of Chicago, early Tuesday, killing two Negroes and beating and robbing several others. In the course of these activities they wantonly destroyed property of white businessmen.

Gangs sprang up as far south as Sixty-third Street in Englewood and in the section west of Wentworth Avenue near Forty-seventh Street. Premeditated depredations were the order of the night. Many Negro homes in mixed districts were attacked, and several of them were burned. Furniture was stolen or destroyed. When raiders were driven off they would return again and again until their designs were accomplished.

The contagion of the race war broke over the boundaries of the South Side and spread to the Italians on the West Side. This community became excited over a rumor, and an Italian crowd killed a Negro, Joseph Lovings.

Wednesday saw a material lessening of crime and violence. The "Black Belt" and the district immediately west of it were still storm centers. But the peak of the rioting had apparently passed, although the danger of fresh outbreaks of magnitude was still imminent. Although companies of the militia had been mobilized in nearby armories as early as Monday night, July 28, it was not until Wednesday evening at 10:30 that the mayor yielded to pressure and asked for their help.

Rain on Wednesday night and Thursday drove idle people of both races into their homes. The temperature fell, and with it the white heat of the riot. From this time on the violence was sporadic, scattered, and meager. The riot seemed well under control, if not actually ended.

Friday witnessed only a single reported injury. At 3:35 A.M. Saturday incendiary fires burned forty-nine houses in the immigrant neighborhood west of the Stock Yards. Nine hundred and forty-eight people, mostly Lithuanians, were made homeless, and the property loss was about $250,000. Responsibility for these fires was never fixed. The riot virtually ceased on Saturday. For the next few days injured were reported occasionally, and by August 8 the riot zone had settled down to normal and the militia was withdrawn. . . .

Outstanding Features of the Riot

This study of the facts of the riot of 1919, the events as they happened hour by hour, the neighborhoods involved, the movements of mobs, the part played by rumors, and the handling of the emergency by the various authorities, shows certain outstanding features which may be listed as follows:

a). The riot violence was not continuous hour by hour, but was intermittent.

b). The greatest number of injuries occurred in the district west and inclusive of Wentworth Avenue, and south of the south branch of the Chicago River to Fifty-fifth Street, or in the Stock Yards district. The next greatest number occurred in the so-called "Black Belt": Twenty-second to Thirty-ninth streets, inclusive, and Wentworth Avenue to the lake, exclusive of Wentworth Avenue; Thirty-ninth to Fifty-fifth streets, inclusive, and Clark Street to Michigan Avenue, exclusive of Michigan Avenue.

c). Organized raids occurred only after a period of sporadic clashes and spontaneous mob outbreaks.

d). Main thoroughfares witnessed 76 per cent of the injuries on the South Side. The streets which suffered most severely were State, Halsted, Thirty-first, Thirty-fifth, and Forty-seventh. Transfer corners were always centers of disturbances.

e). Most of the rioting occurred after work hours among idle crowds on the streets. This was particularly true after the street-car strike began.

f). Gangs, particularly of young whites, formed definite nuclei for crowd and mob formation. "Athletic clubs" supplied the leaders of many gangs.

g). Crowds and mobs engaged in rioting were generally composed of a small nucleus of leaders and an acquiescing mass of spectators. The leaders were mostly young men, usually between the ages of sixteen and twenty-one. Dispersal was most effectively accomplished by sudden, unexpected gun fire.

h). Rumor kept the crowds in an excited, potential mob state. The press was responsible for giving wide dissemination to much of the inflammatory matter in spoken rumors, though editorials calculated to allay race hatred and help the forces of order were factors in the restoration of peace.

i). The police lacked sufficient forces for handling the riot; they were hampered by the Negroes' distrust of them; routing orders and records were not handled with proper care; certain officers were undoubtedly unsuited to police or riot duty.

j). The militiamen employed in this riot were of an unusually high type. This unquestionably accounts for the confidence placed in them by both races. Riot training, definite orders, and good staff work contributed to their efficiency.

k). There was a lack of energetic co-operation between the police department and the state's attorney's office in the discovery and conviction of rioters.

The riot was merely a symptom of serious and profound disorders lying beneath the surface of race relations in Chicago.

30 / Forerunner of "Police Brutality": The "Third Degree," 1931

Police brutality, chiefly against black people, has emerged in recent years as a major issue of debate, but the overzealous questioning and treatment of the accused by police has long been a matter of public concern. In an earlier generation the term was "the third degree" rather than "police brutality." In 1931 the National Commission on Law Observance and Law Enforcement, headed by George W. Wickersham, found the use of the third degree to be widespread.

The Third Degree in America

. . . the third degree—that is, the use of physical brutality, or other forms of cruelty, to obtain involuntary confessions or admissions—is widespread. . . . Physical brutality, illegal detention, and refusal to allow access of counsel to the prisoner is common. . . . Brutality and violence in making an arrest also are employed at times, before the prisoner reaches the jail, in order to put him in a frame of mind which makes him more amenable to questioning afterwards. . . . Several reliable informants in different parts of the country state there is no color discrimination in the application of the third degree, but a few tell us that in their districts these practices are particularly used against Negroes. . . . That the third degree is especially used against the poor and uninfluential is asserted by several writers, and confirmed by official informants and judicial decisions. The likelihood of abuse is less when the prisoner is in contact with an attorney. The poor and uninfluential are less apt to be so represented. But the destitute are not the only victims of the third degree. Cases have been brought to [our] . . . attention of brutal treatment inflicted upon prosperous citizens.

A Black Man Subjected to the Third Degree

In a Texas murder case against a Negro 26 years of age, written and subsequent oral confessions were obtained from him at Marlin and Waco through whippings by the sheriff, who treated at least two witnesses in the same manner. Judge Morrow said, in reversing the conviction:

> He testified that he was commanded by the sheriff to make the statements; that he was denied communication with friends, relatives, or attorneys; that on his arrest the day after the homicide he was brought to the jail in Marlin, and denied any connection with the homicide, and was then whipped by the sheriff, who used a leather

From the *National Commission on Law Observance and Law Enforcement,* Report on Lawlessness in Law Enforcement (*Washington: Government Printing Office, 1931*), pp. 4, 55, 61, 158–160.

strap about 2½ feet long with some strips of leather sewed on the end of it; that he was whipped all over the head, shoulders, and neck, and that there remained scars on his body and head. These scars were exhibited, and testimony relating to them was given by a doctor and another witness. Appellant testified further that the injuries to his arm prevented its use for a month and caused him to swell up so that he could not lie on his side for several months; that he was whipped with the side of the strap and the butt end of it and nearly killed; that when he came to, they were kicking him in the side; that his head still gave pain and swelled up. The swelling was verified by other witnesses. He testified to subsequent whippings in the jail at Marlin and that on one occasion a stick was used by the sheriff which cut the blood and caused an injury from which he had not yet recovered; that he was told by the sheriff to go before the grand jury and make the same statement that he had made to him, otherwise he would be mobbed, and if he did make the same statement he would be discharged after certain white men against whom suspicion rested had been dealt with. In the jail other witnesses, Negroes, were severely and cruelly whipped by the sheriff. One of them was put in water and his head held in water until he was almost drowned. Another, a woman, was stripped of her clothes, laid on the floor, and severely whipped and strapped. Of this the appellant had information. Some of these whippings were manifestly made after the written statement dated July 28, taken at Waco, was signed. All of them were before the statement was given before the grand jury in Marlin in September.

On this hearing the gentleman who was county attorney at the time said: "I was in jail that afternoon and talked to Frank Williams. He was whipped by Mr. Plott in my presence. A strap was used with a wooden handle on it. He was whipped there a little while—I don't know, three, four, or five minutes possibly—I don't know the time. He was not whipped any more that afternoon while I was present. I was present when he was taken from the jail to Waco. After the whipping the Negro said: 'Yes; I did it.' "

A White Man Subjected to the Third Degree

The defendant offered to testify that from about 8:30 in the evening of June 14, when he was arrested, until about noon on June 16, when he was taken to the prosecuting attorney's office, he was sweated almost continuously by various police officers and detectives, who kicked him, beat him with a rubber hose, struck him with a revolver, a chair, and a blackjack, and squeezed and twisted his testicles, and refused to let him sleep and to let him have anything to eat or drink, and threatened to kill him, in their efforts to force him to admit that he actually participated in the robbery and the killing of Officer Smith and to inform them as to others who participated in the perpetration of said crimes; that by means of such mistreatment, torture, threats, and coercion, he was forced, at police headquarters on June 15, to sign the first statement about 9 o'clock in the morning of June 15, and to sign the additional statement some time in the afternoon of that day, without first having an opportunity to read said statements and without having said statements read to him; that, about noon on June 16, he was taken from police headquarters to the prosecuting attorney's office by two detectives, Thurman and Kellerstrauss, who had actively participated in the mistreatment, torture, threats, and coercion to which he had been subjected at police headquarters; that immediately before he was taken into the office of the prosecuting attorney he was told by Thurman that unless, when questioned by the prosecuting attorney, he confirmed the statements signed by him at police headquarters, they (the detectives) would take him back to police headquarters and "finish" him; that Thurman remained in the prosecuting attorney's office throughout his (the defendant's) conversation with the prosecuting attorney; that at the time of said conversation he was suffering from the lack of sleep and food and from the injuries inflicted upon him by said police officers and detectives; and that he confirmed the statements signed by him at police headquarters, when the same were read to him by the prosecuting attorney because he was afraid he would be subjected to further mistreatment and torture at the hands of said police officers and detectives if he did not do so.

31 / Presidential Assassin: Lee Harvey Oswald, Killer of President Kennedy, 1963

On November 22, 1963, President John F. Kennedy was assassinated in Dallas, Texas. Americans of the present generation will never forget the dramatic tragic events of that day and the following ones. After an extensive investigation President Johnson's Commission on the Assassination of President Kennedy, headed by Chief Justice Earl Warren, found that Lee Harvey Oswald was the assassin. The investigation was conducted after Oswald had been fatally shot in the Dallas

From "Lee Harvey Oswald: Background and Possible Motives," Chapter VII of Report of the President's Commission on the Assassination of President John F. Kennedy (*Washington: Government Printing Office, 1964*), pp. 375–80.

police station on November 24 by Jack Ruby. The many critics of the Warren Commission have cited flaws in the Commission's work, but none of the critics has succeeded in seriously undermining the Commission's conclusion that the assassin was Oswald, operating alone.

Like Charles Guiteau and Leon Czolgosz (slayers of Garfield and McKinley respectively, see selections 19 and 25) Oswald had delusions of grandeur. Like Guiteau and Czolgosz, Oswald had a commitment to a political ideology—in Oswald's case, Marxism—which, however, furnished only a superficial motivation. In all three cases, the fundamental reason for the act of assassination seems to have been a deeply rooted mental instability. Like Czolgosz, Oswald was seriously withdrawn in his early years. Like Guiteau, Oswald led an erratic roving adult life and failed in one undertaking after another. The Warren Commission concluded that the basic reason for Oswald's act was his profound sense of alienation from the world in which he lived. This, in turn, stemmed essentially from a childhood and adolescence of severe emotional deprivation. The pattern is one that has often been found in the background of murderers.

The evidence . . . identifies Lee Harvey Oswald as the assassin of President Kennedy and indicates that he acted alone in that event. There is no evidence that he had accomplices or that he was involved in any conspiracy directed to the assassination of the President. There remains the question of what impelled Oswald to conceive and to carry out the assassination of the President of the United States. The Commission has considered many possible motives for the assassination, including those which might flow from Oswald's commitment to Marxism or communism, the existence of some personal grievance, a desire to effect changes in the structure of society or simply to go down in history as a well publicized assassin. None of these possibilities satisfactorily explains Oswald's act if it is judged by the standards of reasonable men. The motives of any man, however, must be analyzed in terms of the character and state of mind of the particular individual involved. For a motive that appears incomprehensible to other men may be the moving force of a man whose view of the world has been twisted, possibly by factors of which those around him were only dimly aware. Oswald's complete state of mind and character are now outside of the power of man to know. He cannot, of course, be questioned or observed by those charged with the responsibility for this report or by experts on their behalf. There is, however, a large amount of material available in his writings and in the history of his life which does give some insight into his character and, possibly, into the motives for his act.

Since Oswald is dead, the Commission is not able to reach any definite conclusions as to whether or not he was "sane" under prevailing legal standards. Under our system of justice no forum could properly make that determination unless Oswald were before it. It certainly could not be made by this Commission which . . . ascertained the facts surrounding the assassination but did not draw conclusions concerning Oswald's legal guilt.

Indications of Oswald's motivation may be obtained from a study of the events, relationships and influences which appear to have been significant in shaping his character and in guiding him. Perhaps the most outstanding conclusion of such a study is that Oswald was profoundly alienated from the world in which he lived. His life was characterized by isolation, frustration, and failure. He had very few, if any, close relationships with other people and he appeared to have great difficulty in finding a meaningful place in the world. He was never satisfied with anything. When he was in the United States he resented the capitalist system which he thought was exploiting him and others like him. He seemed to prefer the Soviet Union and he spoke highly of Cuba. When he was in the Soviet Union, he apparently resented the Communist Party members, who were accorded special privileges and who he thought were betraying communism, and he spoke well of the United States. He accused his wife of preferring others to himself and told her to return to the Soviet Union without him but without a divorce. At the same time he professed his love for her and said that he could not get along without her. Marina Oswald thought that he would not be happy anywhere, "Only on the moon, perhaps."

While Oswald appeared to most of those who knew him as a meek and harmless person, he sometimes imagined himself as "the Commander" and, apparently seriously, as a political prophet—a man who said that after 20 years he would be prime minister. His wife testified that he compared himself with great leaders of history. Such ideas of grandeur were apparently accompanied by notions of oppression. He had a great hostility toward his environment, whatever it happened to be, which he expressed in striking and sometimes violent acts long before the assassination. There was some quality about him that led him to act with an apparent disregard for possible consequences. He defected to the Soviet Union, shot at General Walker, tried to go to Cuba and even contemplated hijacking an airplane to get there. He assassinated the President, shot Officer Tippit, resisted arrest and tried to kill another policeman in the process.

Oswald apparently started reading about communism when he was about 15. In the Marines, he evidenced a strong conviction as to the correctness of Marxist doctrine, which one associate described as "irrevocable," but also as "theoretical"; that associate did not think that Oswald was a Communist. Oswald did not always distinguish between Marxism and communism. He stated several times that he was a Communist but apparently never joined any Communist Party.

His attachment to Marxist and Communist doctrine was probably, in some measure, an expression of his hostility to his environment. While there is doubt about how fully Oswald understood the doctrine which he so often espoused, it seems clear that his commitment to Marxism was an important factor influencing his conduct during his adult years. It was an obvious element in his decision to go to Russia and later to Cuba and it probably influenced his decision to shoot at General Walker. It was a factor which contributed to his character and thereby might have influenced his decision to assassinate President Kennedy.

The discussion below will describe the events known to the Commission which most clearly reveals the formation and nature of Oswald's character. It will attempt to summarize the events of his early life, his experience in New York City and in the Marine Corps, and his interest in Marxism. It will examine his defection to the Soviet Union in 1959, his subsequent return to the United States and his life here after June of 1962. The review of the latter period will evaluate his personal and employment relations, his attempt to kill General Walker, his political activities, and his unsuccessful attempt to go to Cuba in late September of 1963. Various possible motives will be treated in the appropriate context of the discussion outlined above.

The Early Years

Significant in shaping the character of Lee Harvey Oswald was the death of his father, a collector of insurance premiums. This occurred 2 months before Lee was born in New Orleans on October 18, 1939. That death strained the financial fortunes of the remainder of the Oswald family. It had its effect on Lee's mother, Marguerite, his brother Robert, who had been born in 1934, and his half-brother John Pic, who had been born in 1932 during Marguerite's previous marriage. It forced Marguerite Oswald to go to work to provide for her family. Reminding her sons that they were orphans and that the family's financial condition was poor, she placed John Pic and Robert Oswald in an orphans' home. From the time Marguerite Oswald returned to work until December 26, 1942, when Lee too was sent to the orphans' home, he was cared for principally by his mother's sister, by babysitters and by his mother, when she had time for him.

Marguerite Oswald withdrew Lee from the orphans' home and took him with her to Dallas when he was a little over 4 years old. About 6 months later she also withdrew John Pic and Robert Oswald. Apparently that action was taken in anticipation of her marriage to Edwin A. Ekdahl, which took place in May of 1945. In the fall of that year John Pic and Robert Oswald went to a military academy where they stayed, except for vacations, until the spring of 1948. Lee Oswald remained with his mother and Ekdahl, to whom he became quite attached. John Pic testified that he thought Lee found in Ekdahl the father that he never had. That situation, however, was shortlived, for the relations between Marguerite Oswald and Ekdahl were stormy and they were finally divorced, after several separations and reunions, in the summer of 1948.

After the divorce Mrs. Oswald complained considerably about how unfairly she was treated, dwelling on the fact that she was a widow with three children. John Pic, however, did not think her position was worse than that of many other people. In the fall of 1948 she told John Pic and Robert Oswald that she could not afford to send them back to the military school and she asked Pic to quit school entirely to help support the family, which he did for 4 months in the fall of 1948. In order to supplement their income further she falsely swore that Pic was 17 years old so that he could join the Marine Corps Reserves. Pic did turn over part of his income to his mother, but he returned to high school in January of 1949, where he stayed until 3 days before he was scheduled to graduate, when he left school in order to get into the Coast Guard. Since his mother did not approve of his decision to continue school he accepted the responsibility for that decision himself and signed his mother's name to all his own excuses and report cards.

Pic thought that his mother overstated her financial problems and was unduly concerned about money. Referring to the period after the divorce from Ekdahl, which was apparently caused in part by Marguerite's desire to get more money from him, Pic said: "Lee was brought up in this atmosphere of constant money problems, and I am sure it had quite an effect on him, and also Robert." Marguerite Oswald worked in miscellaneous jobs after her divorce from Ekdahl. When she worked for a time as an insurance saleslady, she would sometimes take Lee with her, apparently leaving him alone in the car while she transacted her business. When she worked during the school year, Lee had to leave an empty house in the morning, return to it for lunch and then again at night, his mother having trained him to do that rather than to play with other children.

An indication of the nature of Lee's character at this time was provided in the spring of 1950, when he was sent to New Orleans to visit the family of his mother's sister, Mrs. Lillian Murret, for 2 or 3 weeks. Despite their urgings, he refused to play with the other children his own age. It also appears that Lee tried to tag along with his older brothers but apparently was not able to spend as much time with them as he would have liked, because of the age gaps of 5 and 7 years, which became more significant as the children grew older.

New York City

Whatever problems may have been created by Lee's home life in Louisiana and Texas, he apparently adjusted well enough there to have had an average, although gradually deteriorating, school record with no behavior or truancy problems. That was not the case, however, after he and his mother moved to New York in August of 1952, shortly before Lee's 13th birthday. They moved shortly after Robert joined the Marines; they lived for a time with John Pic who was stationed there with the Coast Guard. Relations soon became strained, however, so in late September Lee and his mother moved to their own apartment in the Bronx. Pic and his wife would have been happy to have kept Lee, however, who was becoming quite a disciplinary problem for his mother, having struck her on at least one occasion.

The short-lived stay with the Pics was terminated after an incident in which Lee allegedly pulled out a pocket knife during an argument and threatened to use it on Mrs. Pic. When Pic returned home, Mrs. Oswald tried to play down the event but Mrs. Pic took a different view and asked the Oswalds to leave. Lee refused to discuss the matter with Pic, whom he had previously idolized, and their relations were strained thereafter.

On September 30, 1952, Lee enrolled in P.S. 117, a junior high school in the Bronx, where the other children apparently teased him because of his "western" clothes and Texas accent. He began to stay away from school, preferring to read magazines and watch television at home by himself. This continued despite the efforts of the school authorities and, to a lesser extent, of his mother to have him return to school. Truancy charges were brought against him alleging that he was "beyond the control of his mother insofar as school attendance is concerned." Lee Oswald was remanded for psychiatric observation to Youth House, an institution in which children are kept for psychiatric observation or for detention pending court appearance or commitment to a child-caring or custodial institution such as a training school. He was in Youth House from April 16 to May 7, 1953, during which time he was examined by its Chief Psychiatrist, Dr. Renatus Hartogs, and interviewed and observed by other members of the Youth House staff.

Marguerite Oswald visited her son at Youth House, where she recalled that she waited in line "with Puerto Ricans and Negroes and everything." She said that her pocketbook was searched "because the children in this home were such criminals, dope fiends, and had been in criminal offenses, that anybody entering this home had to be searched in case the parents were bringing cigarettes or narcotics or anything." She recalled that Lee cried and said, "Mother, I want to get out of here. There are children in here who have killed people, and smoke. I want to get out." Marguerite Oswald said that she had not realized until then in what kind of place her son had been confined.

On the other hand, Lee told his probation officer, John Carro, that "while he liked Youth House he miss[ed] the freedom of doing what he wanted. He indicated that he did not miss his mother." Mrs. Evelyn Strickman Siegel, a social worker who interviewed both Lee and his mother while Lee was confined in Youth House, reported that Lee "confided that the worst thing about Youth House was the fact that he had to be with other boys all the time, was disturbed about disrobing in front of them, taking showers with them, etc."

Contrary to reports that appeared after the assassination, the psychiatric examination did not indicate that Lee Oswald was a potential assassin, potentially dangerous, that "his outlook on life had strongly paranoid overtones" or that he should be institutionalized. Dr. Hartogs did find Oswald to be a tense, withdrawn, and evasive boy who intensely disliked talking about himself and his feelings. He noted that Lee liked to give the impression that he did not care for other people but preferred to keep to himself, so that he was not bothered and did not have to make the effort of communicating. Oswald's withdrawn tendencies and solitary habits were thought to be the result of "intense anxiety, shyness, feelings of awkwardness and insecurity." He was reported to have said "I don't want a friend and I don't like to talk to people" and "I dislike everybody." He was also described as having a "vivid fantasy life, turning around the topics of omnipotence and power, through which he tries to compensate for his present shortcomings and frustrations." Dr. Hartogs summarized his report by stating:

This 13 year old well built boy has superior mental resources and functions only slightly below his capacity level in spite of chronic truancy from school which brought him into Youth House. No finding of neurological impairment or psychotic mental changes could be made. Lee has to be diagnosed as "personality pattern disturbance with schizoid features and passive–aggressive tendencies." Lee has to be seen as an emotionally, quite disturbed youngster who suffers under the impact of really existing emotional isolation and deprivation, lack of affection, absence of family life and rejection by a self involved and conflicted mother.

Dr. Hartogs recommended that Oswald be placed on probation on condition that he seek help and guidance through a child guidance clinic. There, he suggested, Lee should be treated by a male psychiatrist who could substitute for the lack of a father figure. He also recommended that Mrs. Oswald seek "psychotherapeutic guidance through contact with a family agency." The possibility of commitment was to be considered only if the probation plan was not successful.

Lee's withdrawal was also noted by Mrs. Siegel, who described him as a "seriously detached, withdrawn youngster." She also noted that there was "a rather pleasant, appealing quality about this emotionally starved, affectionless youngster which grows as one speaks to him." She thought that he had detached himself from the world around him because "no one in it ever met any of his needs for love." She observed that since Lee's mother worked all day, he made his own meals and spent all his time alone because he didn't make friends with the boys in the neighborhood. She thought that he "withdrew into a completely solitary and detached existence where he did as he wanted and he didn't have to live by any rules or come into contact with people." Mrs. Siegel concluded that Lee "just felt that his mother never gave a damn for him. He always felt like a burden that she simply just had to tolerate." Lee confirmed some of those observations by saying that he felt almost as if there were a veil between him and other people through which they could not reach him, but that he preferred the veil to remain intact. He admitted to fantasies about being powerful and sometimes hurting and killing people, but refused to elaborate on them. He took the position that such matters were his own business. . . .

32 / The Twentieth-Century Race Riot, Commodity Type: The Summer of 1967

Morris Janowitz on the Commodity Race Riot

By the 1960s the commodity riot had become the mode of American racial violence. It is defined below by sociologist Morris Janowitz. (For the earlier "communal" type of race riot, see selection no. 29 in this volume.)

During World War II, the pattern of rioting underwent a transformation which took full form with outbreaks in Harlem and Brooklyn in 1964, in Watts in 1965, and in Newark and Detroit in 1967. For lack of a better term, there has been a metamorphosis from "communal" riots to "commodity" riots. The Detroit riot of 1943 conformed to the communal or contested area pattern. It involved concentrations of recently arrived Negro migrants, and the precipitating incident occurred in a contested area, Belle Isle. The violence spread rapidly and produced clashes between Negroes and whites. However, the Harlem riots of 1943 contained features of the new type of rioting. The Negro population was composed of a higher concentration of long-term residents in the community. Most important, it was a riot that started within the Negro community, not at the periphery. It did not involve a confrontation between white and Negro civilians. It was an outburst against property and retail establishments, plus looting—therefore the notion of the commodity riot in the Negro community. These establishments were mainly owned by outside white proprietors. The deaths and casualties resulted mainly from the use of force against the Negro population by police and National Guard units. Some direct and active participation by white civilians may take place in such a riot, as was the case in Detroit in 1967, but this is a minor element.

From Morris Janowitz, "Patterns of Collective Racial Violence," in Hugh Davis Graham and Ted Robert Gurr, eds., Violence in America: Historical and Comparative Perspectives: A Report to the National Commission on the Causes and Prevention of Violence, 2 vols. (*Washington: Government Printing Office, 1969*), II, 321.

148   *Violence in the Twentieth Century*

Commodity Riots in the Summer of 1967

The wave of commodity riots by black people that began in 1964 in Harlem and Brooklyn hit a new level of explosiveness in the Watts riot of 1965 and reached a peak in the summer of 1967 with massive riots in Newark and Detroit. The shocking volume of riot activity in 1967 (41 major or serious riots, 123 minor ones) represented a national crisis and led President Lyndon B. Johnson to appoint the National Advisory Commission on Civil Disorders, headed by Governor Otto Kerner of Illinois.

Why Did it Happen?

In addressing the question "Why did it happen?" we shift our focus from the local to the national scene, from the particuar events of the summer of 1967 to the factors within the society at large that created a mood of violence among many urban Negroes.

These factors are complex and interacting; they vary significantly in their effect from city to city and from year to year; and the consequences of one disorder, generating new grievances and new demands, become the causes of the next. Thus was created the "thicket of tension, conflicting evidence, and extreme opinions" cited by the President.

Despite these complexities, certain fundamental matters are clear. Of these, the most fundamental is the racial attitude and behavior of white Americans toward black Americans.

Race prejudice has shaped our history decisively; it now threatens to affect our future.

White racism is essentially responsible for the explosive mixture which has been accumulating in our cities since the end of World War II. Among the ingredients of this mixture are:

Pervasive discrimination and segregation in employment, education, and housing, which have resulted in the continuing exclusion of great numbers of Negroes from the benefits of economic progress.

Black in-migration and white exodus, which have produced the massive and growing concentrations of impoverished Negroes in our major

From Report of the National Advisory Commission on Civil Disorders (*Washington: Government Printing Office, 1968*), pp. 5, 73.

cities, creating a growing crisis of deteriorating facilities and services and unmet human needs.

The black ghettos, where segregation and poverty converge on the young to destroy opportunity and enforce failure. Crime, drug addiction, dependency on welfare, and bitterness and resentment against society in general and white society in particular are the result.

At the same time, most whites and some Negroes outside the ghetto have prospered to a degree unparalleled in the history of civilization. Through television and other media, this affluence has been flaunted before the eyes of the Negro poor and the jobless ghetto youth.

Yet these facts alone cannot be said to have caused the disorders. Recently, other powerful ingredients have begun to catalyze the mixture:

Frustrated hopes are the residue of the unfulfilled expectations aroused by the great judicial and legislative victories of the civil rights movement and the dramatic struggle for equal rights in the South.

A climate that tends toward approval and encouragement of violence as a form of protest has been created by white terrorism directed against nonviolent protest; by the open defiance of law and Federal authority by state and local officials resisting desegregation; and by some protest groups engaging in civil disobedience who turn their backs on nonviolence, go beyond the constitutionally protected rights of petition and free assembly, and resort to violence to attempt to compel alteration of laws and policies with which they disagree.

The frustrations of powerlessness have led some Negroes to the conviction that there is no effective alternative to violence as a means of achieving redress of grievances, and of "moving the system." These frustrations are reflected in alienation and hostility toward the institutions of law and government and the white society which controls them, and in the reach toward racial consciousness and solidarity reflected in the slogan "Black Power."

A new mood has sprung up among Negroes, particularly among the young, in which self-esteem and enhanced racial pride are replacing apathy and submission to "the system."

The police are not merely a "spark" factor. To some Negroes police have come to symbolize white power, white racism, and white repression. And the fact is that many police do reflect and express these white attitudes. The atmosphere of hostility and cynicism is reinforced by a widespread belief among Negroes in the existence of police brutality and in a "double standard" of justice and protection—one for Negroes and one for whites.

Patterns of Disorder

. . . The disorders of 1967 were unusual, irregular, complex, and unpredictable social processes. Like most human events, they did not unfold in an orderly sequence. However, an analysis of our survey information leads to some conclusions about the riot process.

In general:

The civil disorders of 1967 involved Negroes acting against local symbols of white American society, authority, and property in Negro neighborhoods—rather than against white persons.

Of 164 disorders reported during the first nine months of 1967, eight (5 percent) were major in terms of violence and damage; 33 (20 percent) were serious but not major; 123 (75 percent) were minor and undoubtedly would not have received national attention as riots had the Nation not been sensitized by the more serious outbreaks.

In the 75 disorders studied by a Senate subcommittee, 83 deaths were reported. Eighty-two percent of the deaths and more than half the injuries occurred in Newark and Detroit. About 10 percent of the dead and 36 percent of the injured were public employees, primarily law officers and firemen. The overwhelming majority of the persons killed or injured in all the disorders were Negro civilians.

Initial damage estimates were greatly exaggerated. In Detroit, newspaper damage estimates at first ranged from $200 to $500 million; the highest recent estimate is $45 million. In Newark, early estimates ranged from $15 to $25 million. A month later damage was estimated at $10.2 million, 80 percent in inventory losses.

In the 24 disorders in 23 cities which we surveyed:

The final incident before the outbreak of disorder, and initial violence itself, generally took place in the evening or at night at a place in which it was normal for many people to be on the streets.

Violence usually occurred almost immediately following the occurrence of the final precipitating incident, and then escalated rapidly. With but few exceptions, violence subsided during the day, and flared rapidly again at night. The night-day cycles continued through the early period of the major disorders.

Disorder generally began with rock and bottle throwing and window breaking. Once store windows were broken, looting usually followed.

Disorder did not erupt as a result of a single "triggering" or "precipitating" incident. Instead, it was generated out of an increasingly disturbed social atmosphere, in which typically a series of tension-heightening incidents over a period of weeks or months became linked in the minds of many in the Negro community with a reservoir of underlying grievances. At some point in the mounting tension, a further incident—in itself often routine or trivial—became the breaking point and the tension spilled over into violence.

"Prior" incidents, which increased tensions and ultimately led to violence, were police actions in almost half the cases; police actions were "final" incidents before the outbreak of violence in 12 of the 24 surveyed disorders.

No particular control tactic was successful in every situation. The varied effectiveness of control techniques emphasizes the need for advance training, planning, adequate intelligence systems, and knowledge of the ghetto community.

Negotiations between Negroes—including young militants as well as older Negro leaders—and white officials concerning "terms of peace" occurred during virtually all the disorders surveyed. In many cases, these negotiations involved discussion of underlying grievances as well as the handling of the disorder by control authorities. . . .

The Profile of a Rioter

The typical rioter in the summer of 1967 was a Negro, unmarried male between the ages of 15 and 24. He was in many ways very different from the stereotype. He was not a migrant. He was born in the state and was a lifelong resident of the city in which the riot took place. Economically his position was about the same as his Negro neighbors who did not actively participate in the riot.

Although he had not, usually, graduated from high school, he was somewhat better educated than the average inner-city Negro, having at least attended high school for a time.

Nevertheless, he was more likely to be working in a menial or low status job as an unskilled laborer. If he was employed, he was not working full time and his employment was frequently interrupted by periods of unemployment.

He feels strongly that he deserves a better job and that he is barred from achieving it, not because of lack of training, ability, or ambition, but because of discrimination by employers.

He rejects the white bigot's stereotype of the Negro as ignorant and shiftless. He takes great pride in his race and believes that in some respects Negroes are superior to whites. He is extremely hostile to whites, but his hostility is more apt to be a product of social and economic class than of race; he is almost equally hostile toward middle class Negroes.

The Newark Riot, July 12-16, 1967

The Newark, New Jersey, riot of July 12–16, 1967, was typical of the commodity riot. Property damage, inflicted largely by blacks, amounted to a staggering $10,251,000. Those killed were mainly blacks (21 out of 23 fatalities)—victims of the riot control tactics of the police, state troopers, and National Guardsmen.

The Precipitating Incident: The Arrest of a Black Cabdriver

Early on the evening of July 12, a cabdriver named John Smith began, according to police reports, tailgating a Newark police car. Smith was an unlikely candidate to set a riot in motion. Forty years old, a Georgian by birth, he had attended college for a year before entering the Army in 1950. In 1953 he had been honorably discharged with the rank of corporal. A chess-playing trumpet player, he had worked as a musician and a factory hand before, in 1963, becoming a cabdriver.

As a cabdriver, he appeared to be a hazard. Within a relatively short period of time he had eight or nine accidents. His license was revoked. When, with a woman passenger in his cab, he was stopped by the police, he was in violation of that revocation.

From the high-rise towers of the Reverend William P. Hayes housing project, the residents can look down on the orange-red brick facade of the Fourth Precinct Police Station and observe every movement. Shortly after 9:30 p.m., people saw Smith, who either refused or was unable to walk, being dragged out of a police car and into the front door of the station.

Within a few minutes, at least two civil rights leaders received calls from a hysterical woman declaring a cabdriver was being beaten by the police. When one of the persons at the station notified the cab company of Smith's arrest, cabdrivers all over the city began learning of it over their cab radios.

Report of the National Advisory Commission on Civil Disorders (*Washington: Government Printing Office, 1968*), pp. 32–35.

A crowd formed on the grounds of the housing project across the narrow street from the station. As more and more people arrived, the description of the beating purportedly administered to Smith became more and more exaggerated. The descriptions were supported by other complaints of police malpractice that, over the years, had been submitted for investigation—but had never been heard of again.

Escalation: The Incident Becomes a Riot

. . . As they were talking to the inspector about initiating an investigation to determine how Smith had been injured, the crowd outside became more and more unruly. Two of the Negro spokesmen went outside to attempt to pacify the people.

There was little reaction to the spokesmen's appeal that the people go home. The second of the two had just finished speaking from atop a car when several Molotov cocktails smashed against the wall of the police station.

With the call of "Fire" most of those inside the station, police officers and civilians alike, rushed out of the front door. The Molotov cocktails had splattered to the ground; the fire was quickly extinguished.

Inspector Melchior had a squad of men form a line across the front of the station. The police officers and the Negroes on the other side of the street exchanged volleys of profanity.

. . . other Negro leaders urged those on the scene to form a line of march toward the city hall.

Some persons joined the line of march. Others milled about in the narrow street. From the dark grounds of the housing project came a barrage of rocks. Some of them fell among the crowd. Others hit persons in the line of march. Many smashed the windows of the police station. The rock throwing, it was believed, was the work of youngsters; approximately 2,500 children lived in the housing project.

Almost at the same time, an old car was set afire in a parking lot. The line of march began to disintegrate. The police, their heads protected by World War I-type helmets, sallied forth to disperse the crowd. A fire engine, arriving on the scene, was pelted with rocks. As police drove people away from the station, they scattered in all directions.

A few minutes later, a nearby liquor store was broken into. Some persons, seeing a caravan of cabs appear at City Hall to protest Smith's arrest, interpreted this as evidence that the disturbance had been organized, and generated rumors to that effect.

However, only a few stores were looted. Within a short period of time the disorder ran its course.

The Riot in Full Swing: July 13–14

On Thursday, inflammatory leaflets were circulated in the neighborhoods of the Fourth Precinct. A "Police Brutality Protest Rally" was announced for early evening in front of the Fourth Precinct Station. Several television stations and newspapers sent news teams to interview people. Cameras were set up. A crowd gathered.

A picket line was formed to march in front of the police station. Between 7 and 7:30 p.m., James Threatt, executive director of the Newark Human Rights Commission, arrived to announce to the people the decision of the mayor to form a citizens group to investigate the Smith incident, and to elevate a Negro to the rank of captain.

The response from the loosely milling mass of people was derisive. One youngster shouted "Black Power!" Rocks were thrown at Threatt, a Negro. The barrage of missiles that followed placed the police station under siege.

After the barrage had continued for some minutes, police came out to disperse the crowd. According to witnesses, there was little restraint of language or action by either side. A number of police officers and Negroes were injured.

As on the night before, once the people had been dispersed, reports of looting began to come in. Soon the glow of the first fire was seen.

Without enough men to establish control, the police set up a perimeter around a 2-mile stretch of Springfield Avenue, one of the principal business districts, where bands of youths roamed up and down smashing windows. Grocery and liquor stores, clothing and furniture stores, drugstores and cleaners, appliance stores and pawnshops were the principal targets. Periodically, police officers would appear and fire their weapons over the heads of looters and rioters. Laden with stolen goods, people began returning to the housing projects.

Near midnight, activity appeared to taper off. The mayor told reporters the city had turned the corner.

As news of the disturbances had spread, however, people had flocked into the streets. As they saw stores being broken into with impunity, many bowed to temptation and joined the looting.

Without the necessary personnel to make mass arrests, police were shooting into the air to clear stores. A Negro boy was wounded by a .22 caliber bullet said to have been fired by a white man riding in a car. Guns were reported stolen from a Sears, Roebuck store. Looting,

fires, and gunshots were reported from a widening area. Between 2
and 2:30 a.m. on Friday, July 14, the mayor decided to request Gov.
Richard J. Hughes to dispatch the state police and National Guard
troops. The first elements of the state police arrived with a sizable
contingent before dawn.

During the morning the Governor and the mayor, together with the
police and National Guard officers, made a reconnaissance of the area.
The police escort guarding the officials arrested looters as they went.
By early afternoon the National Guard had set up 137 roadblocks, and
state police and riot teams were beginning to achieve control. Command of antiriot operations was taken over by the Governor, who de-
creed a "hard line" in putting down the riot.

[By Sunday, July 16, riot activity had tapered off, and on Monday,
July 17, state police and National Guardsmen were evacuated as the
city returned to normal.]

33 / The Business of Violence:
Organized Crime in America, 1967

*"Crime in the streets" and "law and order" have become political
slogans in the 1960s—slogans that, despite frequent misuse by politicians, reflect fundamental social problems and deep-seated public concern. Far less sensational but of equal if not greater significance is the
process by which urban organized crime in America has become a
billion dollar business.*

Organized Crime

Organized crime is a society that seeks to operate outside the control
of the American people and their governments. It involves thousands of
criminals, working within structures as complex as those of any large
corporation, subject to laws more rigidly enforced than those of legitimate governments. Its actions are not impulsive but rather the result
of intricate conspiracies, carried on over many years and aimed at
gaining control over whole fields of activity in order to amass huge
profits.

The core of organized crime activity is the supplying of illegal goods

From The Challenge of Crime in a Free Society: A Report of the President's
Commission on Law Enforcement and Administration of Justice (*Washington:
Government Printing Office, 1967*), *pp. 187–96.*

and services—gambling, loan sharking, narcotics, and other forms of vice—to countless numbers of citizen customers. But organized crime is also extensively and deeply involved in legitimate business and in labor unions. Here it employs illegitimate methods—monopolization, terrorism, extortion, tax evasion—to drive out of control lawful ownership and leadership and to exact illegal profits from the public. And to carry on its many activities secure from governmental interference, organized crime corrupts public officials. . . .

What organized crime wants is money and power. What makes it different from law-abiding organizations and individuals with those same objectives is that the ethical and moral standards the criminals adhere to, the laws and regulations they obey, the procedures they use, are private and secret ones that they devise themselves, change when they see fit, and administer summarily and invisibly. Organized crime affects the lives of millions of Americans, but because it desperately preserves its invisibility many, perhaps most, Americans are not aware how they are affected, or even that they are affected at all. The price of a loaf of bread may go up one cent as the result of an organized crime conspiracy, but a housewife has no way of knowing why she is paying more. If organized criminals paid income tax on every cent of their vast earnings everybody's tax bill would go down, but no one knows how much. . . .

Historical Background

The foothold that organized crime has gained in our society can be partly explained by the belated recognition on the part of the people and their governments of the need for specialized efforts in law enforcement to counter the enterprises and tactics of organized crime. A few law enforcement officials became concerned with the illicit enterprises of Mafia-type groups in the United States near the close of the 19th century. Sustained efforts at investigation were abruptly terminated by the murders of two police officers, one from New Orleans and one from New York City. The multimillion-dollar bootlegging business in the Prohibition era of the 1920's produced intensive investigations by the Treasury Department and the conviction of Chicago racket leader Al Capone.

In the 1930's, the special racket group of Thomas E. Dewey in New York City secured the conviction of several prominent racketeers, including the late Lucky Luciano, the syndicate leader whose organizational genius made him the father of today's confederation of organized crime families. In the early 1940's, FBI investigation of a million-dollar extortion plot in the moving picture industry resulted in the conviction of several racket leaders, including the Chicago family boss who was then a member of organized crime's national council.

After World War II there was little national interest in the problem until 1950, when the U.S. Attorney General convened a national conference on organized crime. This conference made several recommendations concerning investigative and prosecutive needs. Several weeks later the well-publicized hearings of the Senate Special Committee under Senator Kefauver began. The Kefauver committee heard over 800 witnesses from nearly every state and temporarily aroused the concern of many communities. There was a brief series of local investigations in cities where the Senate committee had exposed organized crime operations and public corruption, but law enforcement generally failed to develop the investigative and prosecutive units necessary to root out the activities of the criminal cartels.

In 1957 the discovery of the meeting in Apalachin, N.Y., of at least 75 criminal cartel leaders from every section of the Nation aroused national interest again. This interest was further stimulated by disclosures in the hearings of Senator McClellan's Select Senate Committee investigating organized crime's infiltration of labor and business. A concerted Federal enforcement response developed in the 1950's, and special, institutionalized efforts on the local level have been growing slowly since that time.

La Cosa Nostra ("Our Thing")

Today the core of organized crime in the United States consists of 24 groups operating as criminal cartels in large cities across the Nation. Their membership is exclusively Italian, they are in frequent communication with each other, and their smooth functioning is insured by a national body of overseers. To date, only the Federal Bureau of Investigation has been able to document fully the national scope of these groups, and FBI intelligence indicates that the organization as a whole has changed its name from the Mafia to La Cosa Nostra.

In 1966 J. Edgar Hoover told a House of Representatives Appropriations Subcommittee:

> La Cosa Nostra is the largest organization of the criminal underworld in this country, very closely organized and strictly disciplined. They have committed almost every crime under the sun. . .
>
> La Cosa Nostra is a criminal fraternity whose membership is Italian either by birth or national origin, and it has been found to control

major racket activities in many of our larger metropolitan areas, often working in concert with criminals representing other ethnic backgrounds. It operates on a nationwide basis, with international implications, and until recent years it carried on its activities with almost complete secrecy. It functions as a criminal cartel, adhering to its own body of "law" and "justice" and, in so doing, thwarts and usurps the authority of legally constituted judicial bodies. . .

In individual cities, the local core group may also be known as the "outfit," the "syndicate," or the "mob." These 24 groups work with and control other racket groups, whose leaders are of various ethnic derivations. In addition, the thousands of employees who perform the street-level functions of organized crime's gambling, usury, and other illegal activities represent a cross section of the Nation's population groups.

The present confederation of organized crime groups arose after Prohibition, during which Italian, German, Irish, and Jewish groups had competed with one another in racket operations. The Italian groups were successful in switching their enterprises from prostitution and bootlegging to gambling, extortion, and other illegal activities. They consolidated their power through murder and violence.

Today, members of the 24 core groups reside and are active in [California, Nevada, Arizona, Colorado, Texas, Louisiana, Florida, Missouri, Illinois, Wisconsin, Michigan, Ohio, Pennsylvania, New Jersey, New York, Rhode Island, and Massachusetts]. The scope and effect of their criminal operations and penetration of legitimate businesses vary from area to area. The wealthiest and most influential core groups operate in States including New York, New Jersey, Illinois, Florida, Louisiana, Nevada, Michigan, and Rhode Island. Not shown on the map are many States in which members of core groups control criminal activity even though they do not reside there. For example, a variety of illegal activities in New England is controlled from Rhode Island.

Recognition of the common ethnic tie of the 5,000 or more members of organized crime's core groups is essential to understanding the structure of these groups today. Some have been concerned that past identification of Cosa Nostra's ethnic character has reflected on Italian-Americans generally. This false implication was eloquently refuted by one of the Nation's outstanding experts on organized crime, Sgt. Ralph Salerno of the New York City Police Department. When an Italian-American racketeer complained to him, "Why does it have to be one of your own kind that hurts you?", Sgt. Salerno answered:

I'm not your kind and you're not my kind. My manners, morals, and mores are not yours. The only thing we have in common is that we both spring from an Italian heritage and culture—and you are the traitor to that heritage and culture which I am proud to be part of.

Organized crime in its totality thus consists of these 24 groups allied with other racket enterprises to form a loose confederation operating in large and small cities. In the core groups, because of their permanency of form, strength of organization and ability to control other racketeer operations, resides the power that organized crime has in America today. . . .

Each of the 24 groups is known as a "family," with membership varying from as many as 700 men to as few as 20. Most cities with organized crime have only one family; New York City has five. Each family can participate in the full range of activities in which organized crime generally is known to engage. Family organization is rationally designed with an integrated set of positions geared to maximize profits. Like any large corporation, the organization functions regardless of personnel changes, and no individual—not even the leader—is indispensable. If he dies or goes to jail, business goes on.

The hierarchical structure of the families resembles that of the Mafia groups that have operated for almost a century on the island of Sicily. Each family is headed by one man, the "boss," whose primary functions are maintaining order and maximizing profits. Subject only to the possibility of being overruled by the national advisory group, which will be discussed below, his authority in all matters relating to his family is absolute.

The Infiltration of Legitimate Business

Today, the kinds of production and service industries and businesses that organized crime controls or has invested in range from accounting firms to yeast manufacturing. One criminal syndicate alone has real estate interests with an estimated value of $300 million. In a few instances, racketeers control nationwide manufacturing and service industries with known and respected brand names.

Control of business concerns has usually been acquired through one of four methods: (1) investing concealed profits acquired from gambling and other illegal activities; (2) accepting business interests in payment of the owner's gambling debts; (3) foreclosing on usurious loans; and (4) using various forms of extortion.

Acquisition of legitimate businesses is also accomplished in more sophisticated ways. One organized crime group offered to lend money to a business on condition that a racketeer be appointed to the company's board of directors and that a nominee for the lenders be given first option to purchase if there were any outside sale of the company's stock. Control of certain brokerage houses was secured through foreclosure of usurious loans, and the businesses then used to promote the sale of fraudulent stock, involving losses of more than $2 million to the public.

Criminal groups also satisfy defaulted loans by taking over businesses, hiring professional arsonists to burn buildings and contents, and collecting on the fire insurance. Another tactic was illustrated in the recent bankruptcy of a meatpacking firm in which control was secured as payment for gambling debts. With the original owners remaining in nominal management positions, extensive product orders were placed through established lines of credit, and the goods were immediately sold at low prices before the suppliers were paid. The organized criminal group made a quick profit of three-quarters of a million dollars by pocketing the receipts from sale of the products ordered and placing the firm in bankruptcy without paying the suppliers.

Too little is known about the effects on the economy of organized crime's entry into the business world, but the examples above indicate the harm done to the public and at least suggest how criminal cartels can undermine free competition. The ordinary businessman is hard pressed to compete with a syndicate enterprise. From its gambling and other illegal revenue—on most of which no taxes are paid—the criminal group always has a ready source of cash with which to enter any business. Through union connections, the business run by organized crime either prevents unionization or secures "sweetheart" contracts from existing unions. These tactics are used effectively in combination. In one city, organized crime gained a monopoly in garbage collection by preserving the business's nonunion status and by using cash reserves to offset temporary losses incurred when the criminal group lowered prices to drive competitors out of business.

Strong-arm tactics are used to enforce unfair business policy and to obtain customers. A restaurant chain controlled by organized crime used the guise of "quality control" to insure that individual restaurant franchise holders bought products only from other syndicate-owned businesses. In one city, every business with a particular kind of waste product useful in another line of industry sold that product to a syndicate-controlled business at one-third the price offered by legitimate business.

The cumulative effect of the infiltration of legitimate business in America cannot be measured. Law enforcement officials agree that entry into legitimate business is continually increasing and that it has not decreased organized crime's control over gambling, usury and other profitable, low-risk criminal enterprises.

V

EPILOGUE

The assassinations of Martin Luther King, Jr., and Senator Robert F. Kennedy in the spring of 1968 climaxed a decade of mounting violence and led to a period of national reflection on the continuing problem of violence. One result of this reflection was the appointment by President Lyndon B. Johnson of the National Commission on the Causes and Prevention of Violence under the chairmanship of Dr. Milton S. Eisenhower. Among several task forces of scholars and experts named by the Commission to report to it was one on Historical and Comparative Perspectives, directed by historian Hugh Davis Graham and political scientist Ted Robert Gurr.

34 / A Comparative Perspective: Is America More Violent Than Other Nations?

Whether the United States is now a "violent society" can be answered not in the abstract but only by comparison, either with the American past or with other nations. The historical evidence . . . suggests that we were somewhat more violent toward one another in this decade than we have been in most others, but probably less violent in total magnitude of civil strife than in the latter 19th century, when the turmoil of Reconstruction was followed by massive racial and labor violence. Even so, in contemporary comparison with other nations, acts of collective violence by private citizens in the United States in the last 20 years have been extraordinarily numerous, and this is true also of peaceful demonstrations. In numbers of political assassinations, riots,

From Hugh Davis Graham and Ted Robert Gurr, eds., Violence in America: Historical and Comparative Perspectives: A Report to the National Commission on the Causes and Prevention of Violence, 2 vols. (*Washington: Government Printing Office, 1969*), II, 628–30.

politically relevant armed group attacks, and demonstrations, the United States since 1948 has been among the half-dozen most tumultuous nations in the world. When such events are evaluated in terms of their relative severity, however, the rank of the United States is somewhat lower. The Feierabends and Nesvold have used ranking scales to weigh the severity and numbers of such events during the years from 1948 to 1965, rating peaceful demonstrations as having the least serious impact, civil wars the most serious impact on political systems. In a comparison that gives greatest weight to the frequency of violent events, the United States ranks 14th among 84 nations. In another comparison, based mainly on the severity of all manifestations of political instability, violent or not, the United States stands below the midpoint, 46th among 84 nations. In other words, the United States up to 1965 had much political violence by comparison with other nations but relative stability of its political institutions in spite of it. Paradoxically, we have been a turbulent people but a relatively stable republic.

Some more detailed comparisons are provided by a study of the characteristics of civil strife in 114 nations and colonies in the 1960's. The information on "civil strife" includes all reported acts of collective violence involving 100 or more people; organized private attacks on political targets, whatever the number of participants; and antigovernment demonstrations involving 100 or more people. Three general kinds of civil strife are distinguished: (1) *Turmoil* is relatively spontaneous, partially organized or unorganized strife with substantial popular participation and limited objectives. (2) *Conspiracy* is intensively organized strife with limited participation but with terroristic or revolutionary objectives. (3) *Internal war* is intensively organized strife with widespread participation, always accompanied by extensive and intensive violence and usually directed at the overthrow of political regimes.

The comparisons of the strife study are proportional to population rather than absolute, on grounds that a demonstration by 10,000 of Portugal's 9 million citizens, for example, is more consequential for that nation than a demonstration by the same number of the United States' 200 million citizens is for ours. About 11 of every 1,000 Americans took part in civil strife, almost all of it turmoil, between mid-1963 and mid-1968, compared with an average of 7 per thousand in 17 other Western democracies during the 1961–65 period. Six of these 17 had higher rates of participation than the United States, including Belgium, France, and Italy. About 9,500 reported casualties resulted from American strife, most of them the result of police action. This is a rate of 48 per million population, compared with an average of 12 per million in other Western nations, but American casualties are almost certain to be overreported by comparison with casualties elsewhere. Strife was also of longer duration in the United States than in all but a handful of countries in the world. In total magnitude of strife, taking these three factors into account, the United States ranks first among the 17 Western democracies.

Despite its frequency, civil strife in the United States has taken much less disruptive forms than in many non-Western and some Western countries. More than a million citizens participated in 370 reported civil-rights demonstrations and marches in the 5-year period; almost all of them were peacefully organized and conducted. Of 170 reported antiwar demonstrations, which involved a total of about 700,000 people, the participants initiated violence in about 20. The most extensive violence occurred in 239 recorded hostile outbreaks by Negroes, which resulted in more than 8,000 casualties and 191 deaths. Yet the nation has experienced no internal wars since the Civil War and almost none of the chronic revolutionary conspiracy and terrorism that plague dozens of other nations. The most consequential conspiratorial violence has been white terrorism against blacks and civil-rights workers, which caused some 20 deaths between 1963 and 1968, and black terrorism against whites, mostly the police, which began in 1968.

Although about 220 Americans died in violent civil strife in the 5 years before mid-1968, the rate of 1.1 per million population was infinitesimal compared with the average of all nations of 238 deaths per million, and less than the European average of 2.4 per million. These differences reflect the comparative evidence that, from a worldwide perspective, Americans have seldom organized for violence. Most demonstrators and rioters are protesting, not rebelling. If there were many serious revolutionaries in the United States, or effective revolutionary organizations, levels of violence would be much higher than they have been.

These comparisons afford little comfort when the tumult of the United States is contrasted with the relative domestic tranquillity of developed democratic nations like Sweden, Great Britain, and Australia, or with the comparable current tranquillity of nations as diverse as Yugoslavia, Turkey, Jamaica, or Malaysia. In total magnitude of strife, the United States ranks 24th among the 114 larger nations and colonies of the world. In magnitude of turmoil alone, it ranks sixth.

Though greater in magnitude, civil strife in the United States is about the same in kind as strife in other Western nations. The antigovernment demonstration and riot, violent clashes of political or ethnic groups, and student protests are pervasive forms of conflict in modern democracies. Some such public protest has occurred in every Western nation in the past decade. People in non-Western countries also resort to these limited forms of public protest, but they are much more likely to organize serious conspiratorial and revolutionary movements as well. Strife in the United States and other European countries is quite likely to mobilize members of both the working class and middle classes, but rarely members of the political establishment such as military officers, civil servants, and disaffected political leaders, who so often organize conspiracies and internal wars in non-European nations. Strife also is likely to occur within or on the periphery of the normal political process in Western nations, rather than being organized by clandestine revolutionary movements or cells of plotters. If some overt strife is an inevitable accompaniment of organized social existence, as all our comparative evidence suggests it is, it seems socially preferable that it take the form of open political protest, even violent protest, rather than concerted, intensively violent attempts to seize political power.

One evident characteristic of civil strife in the United States in recent years is the extent to which it is an outgrowth of ethnic tensions. Much of the civil protest and collective violence in the United States has been directly related to the nation's racial problems. Comparative studies show evidence of parallel though not identical situations in other developed, European, and democratic nations. The unsatisfied demands of regional, ethnic, and linguistic groups for greater rights and socioeconomic benefits are more common sources of civil strife in Western nations than in almost any other group of countries. These problems have persisted long after the resolution of fundamental questions about the nature of the state, the terms of political power and who should hold it, and economic development. It seems ironical that nations that have been missionaries of technology and political organization to the rest of the world apparently have failed to provide satisfactory conditions of life for all the groups within their midst.

35 / An Historical Perspective: Does Violence Succeed?

For all our rhetoric, we have never been a very law-abiding nation, and illegal violence has sometimes been abundantly rewarded. Hence there have developed broad normative sanctions for the expression or acting out of discontent, somewhat limited inhibitions, and—owing to

From Graham and Gurr, eds., Violence in America . . . , *II, 634–38.*

Jeffersonian liberalism's legacy of fear of central public authority—
very circumscribed physical controls. Public sympathy has often been
with the lawbreaker—sometimes with the nightrider who punished
the transgressor of community mores, sometimes with the integration-
ists who refused to obey racial segregation laws. Lack of full respect
for law and support for violence in one's own interest have both contributed to the justifications for private violence, justifications that in
turn have helped make the United States historically and at present a
tumultuous society.

On the other hand, the United States also has characteristics that in
other countries appear to minimize intense revolutionary conspiracies
and internal wars. Thus far in our history the American political system has maintained a relatively high degree of legitimacy in the eyes
of most of its citizens. American political and economic institutions are
generally strong. They are not pervasive enough to provide adequate
opportunities for some regional and minority groups to satisfy their
expectations, but sufficiently pervasive and egalitarian that the most
ambitious and talented men—if not women—can pursue the "American dream" with some chance of success. These are conditions that
minimize the prospects of revolutionary movements: a majoritarian
consensus on the legitimacy of government, and provision of opportunity for men of talent who, if intensely alienated, might otherwise
provide revolutionary cadres. But if such a system is open to the majority yet partly closed to a minority, or legitimate for the majority
but illegitimate for a minority, the minority is likely to create chronic
tumult even though it cannot organize effective revolutionary movements. . . .

Does violence succeed? The inheritors of the doctrines of Frantz
Fanon and "Ché" Guevara assert that if those who use it are sufficiently dedicated, revolution can always be accomplished. Many vehe-
ment advocates of civil order and strategists of counterinsurgency hold
essentially the same faith: that sufficient use of public violence will
deter private violence. This fundamental agreement of "left" and
"right" on the effectiveness of force for modifying others' behavior is
striking. But to what extent is it supported by theory and by historical
evidence?

The two most fundamental human responses to the use of force are
to flee or to fight. This assertion rests on rather good psychological
and ethological evidence about human and animal aggression. Force
threatens and angers men, especially if they believe it to be illegitimate
or unjust. Threatened, they will defend themselves if they can, flee if
they cannot. Angered, they have an innate disposition to retaliate in

kind. Thus men who fear assault attempt to arm themselves, and two-thirds or more of white Americans think that black looters and arsonists should be shot. Governments facing violent protest often regard compromise as evidence of weakness and devote additional resources to counterforce. Yet if a government responds to the threat or use of violence with greater force, its effects in many circumstances are identical with the effects that dictated its actions: its opponents will if they can resort to greater force.

There are only two inherent limitations on such an escalating spiral of force and counterforce: the exhaustion of one side's resources for force, or the attainment by one of the capacity for genocidal victory. There are societal and psychological limitations as well, but they require tacit bonds between opponents: one's acceptance of the ultimate authority of the other, arbitration of the conflict by neutral authority, recognition of mutual interest that makes bargaining possible, or the perception that acquiesence to a powerful opponent will have less harmful consequences than resisting to certain death. In the absence of such bases for cooperation, regimes and their opponents are likely to engage in violent conflict to the limit of their respective abilities.

To the extent that this argument is accurate, it suggests one kind of circumstance in which violence succeeds: that in which one group so overpowers its opponents that they have no choice short of death but to desist. When they do resist to the death, the result is a Carthaginian peace. History records many instances of successful uses of overpowering force. Not surprisingly, the list of successful governmental uses of force against opponents is much longer than the list of dissident successes against government, because most governments have much greater capacities for force, provided they keep the loyalty of their generals and soldiers. Some dissident successes discussed in this volume include the French, American, Nazi, and Cuban Revolutions. Some governmental successes include, in Britain, the suppression of the violent phases of the Luddite and Chartist movements in the 19th century; in Venezuela the Betancourt regime's elimination of revolutionary terrorism; in the United States the North's victory in the Civil War, and the quelling of riots and local rebellions, from the Whiskey Rebellion of 1794 to the ghetto riots of the 1960's.

Governmental uses of force are likely to be successful in quelling specific outbreaks of private violence except in those rare circumstances when the balance of force favors its opponents, or the military defects. But the historical evidence also suggests that governmental violence often succeeds only in the short run. The government of Imperial Russia quelled the revolution of 1905, but in doing so intensified the hostilities of its opponents, who mounted a successful revolution 12 years later, after the government was weakened by a protracted and unsuccessful war. The North "won" the Civil War, but in its very triumph created hostilities that contributed to one of the greatest and most successful waves of vigilante violence in our history. The 17,000 Klansmen of the South today are neither peaceable nor content with the outcome of the "War of Northern Aggression." State or federal troops have been dispatched to quell violent or near-violent labor conflict in more than 160 recorded instances in American history; they were immediately successful in almost every case yet did not significantly deter subsequent labor violence.

The long-range effectiveness of governmental force in maintaining civil peace seems to depend on three conditions identified by the papers in this volume: public belief that governmental use of force is legitimate, consistent use of that force, and remedial action for the grievances that give rise to private violence. The decline of violent working-class protest in 19th century England was predicated on an almost universal popular acceptance of the legitimacy of the government, accompanied by the development of an effective police system —whose popular acceptance was enhanced by its minimal reliance on violence—and by gradual resolution of working class grievances. The Cuban case was quite the opposite: the governmental response to private violence was terroristic, inconsistent public violence that alienated most Cubans from the Batista regime, with no significant attempts to reduce the grievances, mostly political, that gave rise to rebellion.

We have assumed that private violence is "successful" in those extreme cases in which a government capitulates in the face of the superiority of its opponents. This is not the only or necessarily the best criterion of "success," though. A better criterion is the extent to which the grievances that give rise to collective protest and violence are resolved. Even revolutionary victories do not necessarily lead to complete success in these terms. The American Revolution returned effective political control to the hands of the colonists, but eventually led to an expansion of state and federal authority that diminished local autonomy to the point that new rebellions broke out in many frontier areas over essentially the same kinds of grievances that had caused the revolution. The Bolshevik revolution ended Russia's participation in World War I, which was perhaps the greatest immediate grievance of the Russian people, and in the long run brought great economic and social benefits; but the contingent costs of the subsequent civil war, famine, and totalitarian political control were enormous. The middle-class political discontents that fueled the Cuban revolutionary movement, far from being remedied, were intensified when the revolutionary leaders used their power to effect a basic socioeconomic reconstruction of society that favored themselves and the rural working classes.

If revolutionary victory is unlikely in the modern state, and uncertain of resolving the grievances that give rise to revolutionary movements, are there any circumstances in which less intensive private violence is successful? We said above that the legitimacy of governmental force is one of the determinants of its effectiveness. The same principle applies to private violence: It can succeed when it is widely regarded as legitimate. The vigilante movements of the American frontier had widespread public support as a means for establishing order in the absence of adequate law enforcement agencies, and were generally successful. The Ku Klux Klan of the Reconstruction era similarly had the sympathy of most white Southerners and was largely effective in reestablishing and maintaining the prewar social and political status quo. The chronicles of American labor violence, however, suggest that violence was almost always ineffective for the workers involved. In a very few instances there was popular and state governmental support for the grievances of workers that had led to violent confrontations with employers, and in several of these cases state authority was used to impose solutions that favored the workers. But in the great majority of cases the public and officials did not accept the legitimacy of labor demands, and the more violent was conflict, the more disastrous were the consequences for the workers who took part. Union organizations involved in violent conflict seldom gained recognition, their supporters were harassed and often lost their jobs, and tens of thousands of workers and their families were forcibly deported from their homes and communities.

The same principle applies, with two qualifications, to peaceful public protest. If demonstrations are regarded as a legitimate way to express grievances, and if the grievances themselves are widely held to be justified, protest is likely to have positive effects. One of the qualifications is that if public opinion is neutral on an issue, protest demonstrations can have favorable effects. This appears to have been an initial consequence of the civil-rights demonstrations of the early 1960's in the North. If public opinion is negative, however, demonstrations are likely to exacerbate popular hostility. During World War I, for example, pacifist demonstrators were repeatedly attacked, beaten, and in some cases lynched, with widespread public approval and sometimes official sanction. Contemporary civil-rights demonstrations and activities in the South and in some northern cities have attracted similar responses.

The second qualification is that when violence occurs during protest activities, it is rather likely to alienate groups that are not fundamentally in sympathy with the protesters. We mentioned above the unfavorable consequences of labor violence for unions and their members, despite the fact that violence was more often initiated by employers than by workers. In the long run, federally enforced recognition and bargaining procedures were established, but this occurred only after labor violence had passed its climacteric, and moreover in circumstances in which no union leaders advocated violence. In England, comparably, basic political reforms were implemented not in direct response to Chartist protest, but long after its violent phase had passed.

The evidence supports one basic principle: Force and violence can be successful techniques of social control and persuasion when they have extensive popular support. If they do not, their advocacy and use are ultimately self-destructive, either as techniques of government or of opposition. The historical and contemporary evidence of the United States suggests that popular support tends to sanction violence in support of the status quo: the use of public violence to maintain public order, the use of private violence to maintain popular conceptions of social order when government cannot or will not. If these assertions are true—and not much evidence contradicts them—the prolonged use of force or violence to advance the interests of any segmental group may impede and quite possibly preclude reform. This conclusion should not be taken as an ethical judgement, despite its apparent correspondence with the "establishmentarian" viewpoint. It represents a fundamental trait of American and probably all mankind's character, one which is ignored by advocates of any political orientation at the risk of broken hopes, institutions, and lives.

Further Readings

The most complete treatment of American violence yet published is a volume of interdisciplinary essays, *The History of Violence in America: Historical and Comparative Perspectives,* edited by Hugh Davis Graham and Ted Robert Gurr (New York: Frederick A. Praeger, 1969). This study was first published under the title of *Violence in America: Historical and Comparative Perspectives: A Report to the National Commission on the Causes and Prevention of Violence,* 2 vols. (Washington: Government Printing Office, 1969) and was reprinted in single volume paperback editions in 1969 by Bantam Books and Signet. One of the essays included is Richard Maxwell Brown, "Historical Patterns of Violence in America," a brief but quite comprehensive survey whose notes constitute a select bibliography of the history of American violence. For further reading on the history of American violence, the reader is directed to the following items, as well as to the full text of the works cited as sources for the documents in this volume.

Adamic, Louis. *Dynamite: The Story of Class Violence in America.* New York, 1934.

Adams, Graham, Jr. *Age of Industrial Violence, 1910–1915.* New York, 1966. (28)[1]

Alexander, Charles C. *The Ku Klux Klan in the Southwest.* Lexington, Kentucky, 1965.

Altman, Jack and Ziporyn, Marvin C. *Born to Raise Hell: The Untold Story of Richard Speck.* New York, 1967.

Andrews, Charles M., ed. *Narratives of the Insurrections, 1675–1690.* New York, 1915. (2)

Angle, Paul M. *Bloody Williamson: A Chapter in American Lawlessness.* New York, 1952.

Aptheker, Herbert. *American Negro Slave Revolts.* New York, 1943.

Asbury, Herbert. *The Gangs of New York.* New York, 1928.

Baldwin, Leland D. *Whiskey Rebels.* Pittsburgh, 1939.

Bancroft, Hubert Howe. *Popular Tribunals.* 2 vols. San Francisco, 1887.

Birney, Hoffman. *Vigilantes.* Philadelphia, 1929. (12)

Bishop, James A. *The Day Kennedy Was Shot.* New York, 1968. (31)

---

[1] A number in parentheses after one of the items indicates that it is especially recommended for further reading in regard to the document of that number in this book.

Broehl, Wayne, G., Jr. *The Molly Maguires.* Cambridge, Massachusetts, 1964. (16)

Brown, Richard Maxwell. "The American Vigilante Tradition." In *History of Violence in America,* edited by Hugh Davis Graham and Ted Robert Gurr. New York, 1969.

Brown, Richard Maxwell. *The South Carolina Regulators.* Cambridge, Massachusetts, 1963. (5)

Brownlee, Richard S. *Grey Ghosts of the Confederacy: Guerrilla Warfare in the West, 1861–1865.* Baton Rouge, Louisiana, 1958.

Bruce, Robert V. *1877: Year of Violence.* Indianapolis, 1959. (18)

Capote, Truman. *In Cold Blood.* New York, 1966.

Caughey, John W., ed. *Their Majesties the Mob.* Chicago, 1960.

Chalmers, David M. *Hooded Americanism: The First Century of the Ku Klux Klan, 1865–1965.* Garden City, New York, 1965.

Christman, Henry. *Tin Horns and Calico.* New York, 1945. (9)

Clark, John H., ed. *William Styron's Nat Turner: Ten Black Writers Respond.* Boston, 1968. (8)

Coates, Robert M. *The Outlaw Years: The History of the Land Pirates of the Natchez Trace.* New York, 1930.

Coxe, John E. "The New Orleans Mafia Incident." *Louisiana Historical Quarterly,* October, 1937. (23)

Cressey, Donald R. *Theft of the Nation: The Structure and Operation of Organized Crime in America.* New York, 1969. (33)

David, Henry. *The History of the Haymarket Affair.* New York, 1936.

Davis, David B. *Homicide in American Fiction, 1789–1860.* Ithaca, New York, 1957.

Deutsch, Hermann B. *The Huey Long Murder Case.* Garden City, New York, 1963.

Drewry, William S. *The Southampton Insurrection.* Washington, 1900. (8)

Dykstra, Robert R. *The Cattle Towns.* New York, 1968.

Ellis, David. *Landlords and Farmers in the Hudson-Mohawk Region, 1790–1850.* Ithaca, New York, 1946. (9)

Forrest, Earle R. *Arizona's Dark and Bloody Ground.* Caldwell, Idaho, 1936.

Fulton, Maurice G. *History of the Lincoln County War.* Tucson, Arizona, 1968.

Gard, Wayne. *Frontier Justice.* Norman, Oklahoma, 1949.

Gibson, Arrell M. *The Life and Death of Colonel Albert Jennings Fountain.* Norman, Oklahoma, 1965.

Handlin, Oscar. *Boston's Immigrants.* New York, 1968. (7)

Headley, Joel T. *The Great Riots of New York, 1712 to 1783.* New York, 1873. (7)

Holbrook, Stewart H. *The Rocky Mountain Revolution.* New York, 1965. (26)

Horan, James D. *The Pinkertons.* New York, 1968.

Horn, Stanley F. *Invisible Empire: The Story of the Ku Klux Klan, 1866–1871.* Boston, 1939. (15)

Jones, Virgil C. *The Hatfields and the McCoys.* Chapel Hill, North Carolina, 1948. (17)

Jordan, Winthrop D. *White Over Black: American Attitudes Toward the Negro, 1550–1812.* Chapel Hill, North Carolina, 1968.

Labaree, Benjamin W. *The Boston Tea Party.* New York, 1964. (6)

Lane, Roger. *Policing the City: Boston, 1822–1885.* Cambridge, Massachusetts, 1967.

Leach, Douglas E. *Flintlock and Tomahawk: New England in King Philip's War.* New York, 1966.

Leiby, Adrian C. *The Revolutionary War in the Hackensack Valley.* New Brunswick, New Jersey, 1962.

Lemisch, Jesse. "Jack Tar in the Streets. . . ." *William and Mary Quarterly,* 3rd series, July, 1968. (4)

McCague, James. *The Second Rebellion.* New York, 1968. (11)

Maier, Pauline. "Popular Uprisings and Civil Authority in Eighteenth Century America." *William and Mary Quarterly,* 3rd series, January, 1970.

Manchester, William R. *The Death of a President, November 20–November 25, 1963.* New York, 1967. (31)

Miller, Nyle H. and Snell, Joseph W. *Why the West Was Wild.* Topeka, Kansas, 1963.

Morgan, Edmund S. and Helen M. *The Stamp Act: Prologue to Revolution.* Chapel Hill, North Carolina, 1953. (6)

Morris, Lucile. *Bald Knobbers.* Caldwell, Idaho, 1939.

Nall, James O. *The Tobacco Night Riders of Kentucky and Tennessee, 1905–1909.* Louisville, 1939. (27)

Nordyke, Lewis. *John Wesley Hardin, Texas Gunman.* New York, 1957. (14)

Raper, Arthur F. *The Tragedy of Lynching.* Chapel Hill, North Carolina, 1938. (24)

Roddis, Louis H. *The Indian Wars of Minnesota.* Cedar Rapids, Iowa, 1956. (10)

Rosenberg, Charles E. *The Trial of the Assassin Guiteau.* Chicago, 1968. (19)

Rudolph, Lloyd I. "The Eighteenth Century Mob in Europe and America." *American Quarterly,* Winter, 1959.

Rudwick, Elliot M. *Race Riot at East St. Louis: July 2, 1917.* Carbondale, Illinois, 1964.

Shover, John L. *Cornbelt Rebellion: The Farmers' Holiday Association.* Urbana, Illinois, 1965.

Smith, Helena Huntington. *The War on Powder River.* New York, 1966.

Sonnichsen, C[harles] L. *I'll Die Before I'll Run.* New York, 1961.

Sonnichsen, C[harles] L. *Ten Texas Feuds.* Albuquerque, New Mexico, 1957.

Starkey, Marion L. *A Little Rebellion* [Shay's Rebellion]. New York, 1955.

Styron, William. *The Confessions of Nat Turner.* New York, 1967. (8)

Taft, Philip and Ross, Philip. "American Labor Violence: Its Causes, Character, and Outcome." In *History of Violence in America,* edited by Hugh Davis Graham and Ted Robert Gurr. New York, 1969.

Warner, Sam Bass, Jr. *The Private City: Philadelphia in Three Periods of Its Growth.* Philadelphia, 1968. (7)

Warren, Robert Penn. *Night Rider.* Boston, 1939. (27)

Washburn, Wilcomb E. *The Governor and the Rebel: A History of Bacon's Rebellion in Virginia.* Chapel Hill, North Carolina, 1957.

Waskow, Arthur I. *From Race Riot to Sit-In, 1919 and the 1960's.* Garden City, New York, 1966. (29)

Webb, Walter Prescott. *The Texas Rangers.* Boston, 1935.

Wellman, Paul I. *A Dynasty of Western Outlaws.* New York, 1961.

Wellman, Paul I. *Indian Wars of the West.* Garden City, New York, 1954.

White, Walter. *Rope & Faggot.* New York, 1929. (24)

Williams, Mary Floyd. *History of the San Francisco Committee of Vigilance 1851.* Berkeley, California, 1921.

Wolff, Leon. *Lockout: The Story of the Homestead Strike of 1892.* New York, 1965.

Yellen, Samuel. *American Labor Struggles.* New York, 1936.